Me 163
VS
ALLIED HEAVY BOMBERS

Northern Europe 1944–45

ROBERT FORSYTH

OSPREY PUBLISHING
Bloomsbury Publishing Plc
Kemp House, Chawley Park, Cumnor Hill, Oxford, OX2 9PH, UK
29 Earlsfort Terrace, Dublin 2, Ireland
1385 Broadway, 5th Floor, New York, NY 10018, USA
E-mail: info@ospreypublishing.com
www.ospreypublishing.com

OSPREY is a trademark of Osprey Publishing Ltd

First published in Great Britain in 2024

A catalogue record for this book is available from the British Library.

ISBN: PB 9781472861856; eBook 9781472861870; ePDF 9781472861887;
XML 9781472861863

24 25 26 27 28 10 9 8 7 6 5 4 3 2 1

Edited by Tony Holmes
Cover artwork and battlescene by Gareth Hector
Three-views, side-views, cockpit view, Engaging the Enemy and armament
views by Jim Laurier
Map and tactical diagram by www.bounford.com
Index by Angela Hall
Typeset by PDQ Digital Media Solutions, Bungay, UK
Printed and bound in India by Replika Press Private Ltd.

Osprey Publishing supports the Woodland Trust, the UK's leading woodland
conservation charity.

To find out more about our authors and books visit www.ospreypublishing.com.
Here you will find extracts, author interviews, details of forthcoming events,
and the option to sign up for our newsletter.

Acknowledgments

My grateful thanks, first and foremost, are due to Stephen Ransom and the
late Hans-Hermann Camman, with whom it was my privilege to work on
their own exhaustive and meticulous study of the Me 163. I am glad that some
of the Allied veterans whom I was able to locate at that time have their stories
told here again. I must also thank Eddie Creek, Andy Thomas, Robert Wilde-
Evans at Spink & Son, Larry Milberry and Tony Holmes for their kind
contributions.

B-17 Flying Fortress cover artwork

B-17G 42-31636 *OUT HOUSE MOUSE* of the 323rd BS/91st BG was one
of five Flying Fortresses to be attacked by Me 163s during a raid by the
USAAF's Eighth Air Force on synthetic oil refineries in central Germany on
August 16, 1944. The bomber is believed to have been damaged as a result of
a firing pass made by Leutnant Hartmut Ryll of 1./JG 400. Flown by 1Lt
Reese Walker "Moon" Mullins, *OUT HOUSE MOUSE* had been attacked and
damaged by Bf 109s and an Fw 190 earlier in the mission, leaving it a
"straggler." At 1045 hrs, Ryll carried out a glide attack from "six o'clock high"
that left two of the B-17's crew wounded. *OUT HOUSE MOUSE* had arrived
in Britain on December 11, 1943 and was assigned to the 91st BG at
Bassingbourn on March 12, 1944. After its encounter with the Luftwaffe
fighters, the bomber was repaired and eventually returned to the USA in late
May 1945, having completed 139 missions. It was not scrapped until 1963.
(Artwork by Gareth Hector)

Me 163 cover artwork

Me 163B V53 Wk-Nr 16310062 was flown into combat in early August 1944
by Unteroffizier Kurt Schiebeler of Brandis-based 1./JG 400. It is quite
possible that both Schiebeler and this aircraft may have been deployed against
the USAAF mission targeting the oil refineries on August 16. In his logbook,
Schiebeler noted that he also made an unsuccessful attempt to attack a B-17
on August 24, but he accounted for another shot down – his first – on
September 11, believed to have been from the 100th BG. Schiebeler flew his
last sortie in the Me 163 on November 2, 1944. Built by Klemm Technik in
Stuttgart-Böblingen, the aircraft illustrated here, coded GH+IV, is known to
have been air-towed and flight-tested at Jesau on June 25, 1944. Following
service with 1./JG 400, it was transferred to EJG 1 for instructional purposes.
(Artwork by Gareth Hector)

Previous Page

Stettin-born Feldwebel Siegfried Schubert of 1./JG 400 photographed in the
cockpit of an Me 163, seemingly unperturbed by the prospect of smoking a
pipe while surrounded by highly volatile *T-* and *C-Stoff.* Schubert scored the
first of his *Staffel's* victories on August 16, 1944, but was to lose his life in
combat on October 7. (Ransom Collection)

CONTENTS

INTRODUCTION

On May 10, 1935, in a room somewhere within the cavernous and austere concrete walls of the new *Reichsluftministerium* (RLM – Reich Air Ministry) in Berlin, two men sat facing each other across a desk. One, the "host," wearing the uniform of the nascent Luftwaffe, was Major Wolfram *Freiherr* von Richthofen, a qualified engineer and the head of Department LC II within the RLM's Technical Office. As such, von Richthofen was in charge of research and development of new airframes and aero engines at the armed forces' secret test centers. The other officer was Hauptmann Leo Zanssen, a ballistics and munitions specialist from the *Heereswaffenamt* (HWA – Army Ordnance Office). Von Richthofen was aware that the army had been involved in the development of rocket propulsion for missiles and artillery weapons, and wanted to know if such a means of propulsion could be integrated into development work being undertaken by the Junkers aircraft company.

To the RLM, the attraction of the still relatively new means of rocket propulsion was that aircraft powered in such a way would have the capability of being able to intercept high-altitude enemy bombers within a short period of time. Von Richthofen was particularly attuned to the real threat of new generations of enemy bombers being able to fly at altitudes above 10,000m – a height which would make them immune to existing air defenses.

Although it had been some 15 years since the influential Italian air power theorist Marshal Guilio Douhet had prophesied the invincibility of mass formations of heavily armed "fleets" of bombers able to wreak destruction on an enemy's civilian population and its industries, the specter of such threat continued to haunt the corridors of the world's air ministries. The British Conservative politician Stanley Baldwin stated in late 1932 that "No power on earth can protect the man in the street from being bombed. Whatever people may tell him, the bomber will always get through."

However, the prospect of rocket power for aircraft, in one form or another, was not new to Germany's generals and aircraft designers. During the 1920s Junkers had conducted trials with solid-propellant rockets intended to offer take-off boost to heavily laden aircraft, and on July 25, 1929, a Junkers W 34 seaplane took off from the River Elbe assisted by wing-mounted powder rocket units manufactured by the J. F. Eisfeld company. Representatives from Junkers had been present the year before to observe tests which Austrian rocket pioneer and author on space exploration Max Valier undertook with small, unmanned rail-bound vehicles in the wake of successful trials with a rocket-powered car made by Opel. The Junkers team was sufficiently impressed to continue further tests with Eisfeld rockets, as well as ordering improved variants intended for aircraft take-off assistance.

Evidently things had progressed by August 4, 1932, for a report written by Philipp von Döpp, Junkers' head of aerodynamics, on that date contained a sketch of a proposed single-seat, rocket-powered fighter designed to attack fleets of enemy bombers at altitudes up to 15,000m. The design incorporated a jettisonable cockpit for the pilot, five bi-propellant rocket motors and two machine guns installed alongside a landing skid. By April 1935, shortly before the meeting between von Richthofen and Zanssen, this project had been refined to include a single engine fuelled by liquid methane and liquid oxygen.

The army, however, remained circumspect about cooperation with the Luftwaffe. So secret was rocket development, that 12 days after von Richthofen met Zanssen, the *Reichswehrminister* wrote to the RLM stating that while he could see that the current status of army development justified further exploration of rocket power for aircraft, "collaboration between the HWA and Junkers could be possible only if secrecy surrounding further trials and the design of a rocket engine is guaranteed." The

The sleek form of the Opel-RAK 2 "winged" rocket car, driven by Kurt C. Volkhart, streaks past spectators at the AVUS (Automobil-Verkehrs- und Übungsstraße) test track in Berlin on May 23, 1928. The car was powered by 24 Brander cluster powder rocket propulsion units and reached 230km/h. (Ransom Collection)

Reichswehrminister further opined that a small, specialist team be set up by Junkers for this purpose and "segregated from the rest of the enterprise."

Meanwhile, just over two months later on July 28, 1935, and 5,000 miles away in Seattle, Washington, a large four-engined aircraft took off from Boeing's plant on its maiden flight. Based on a commercial airliner design, the 100ft-wingspan Model 299 was powered by four 750hp Pratt & Whitney R-1690-E Hornet nine-cylinder air-cooled radial engines and featured four blister-type flexible machine gun stations, each of which could accommodate a 0.30-cal. or 0.50-cal. machine gun. An additional station for a nose machine gun was incorporated, and a bomb load of up to eight 600lb bombs could be carried internally. It is popularly believed that upon observing the aircraft for the first time that day, one impressed newspaper reporter commented that the bomber had the appearance of a "flying fortress."

The origins of this aircraft lay in a US Army Air Corps (USAAC) tender of August 8, 1934 which called for a multi-engined, long-range bomber capable of delivering a one-ton bomb load. The aircraft had to be capable of attaining a speed of 250mph, a range of 2,000 miles and an operating ceiling of 10,000ft. The tender-winning company could expect to be rewarded with an order for 200 such aircraft.

Boeing submitted its design to the USAAC as the Model X-299, later amended to B-299. The specification and performance of the prototype fared well against competing designs from Martin and Douglas. However, an ensuing crash during testing at Wright Field, in Dayton, Ohio, in which Boeing test pilot Leslie Tower and Maj Ployer P. Hill, the chief of Wright Field's Flight-Testing Section, were killed, almost ended further work on the B-299. Despite this setback, in January 1936, in an apparent about-turn, the USAAC placed an order for 13 new test models under the designation Y1B-17 (the "Y" denoting aircraft that were undergoing service testing

Guarding the skies. A formation of six Y1B-17s of the 2nd BG fly over the Manhattan skyline and the Hudson River in February 1938. The aircraft were heading for Buenos Aires on a long-distance proving flight. (Author's Collection)

6

prior to acceptance) which were to be assigned to the 2nd BG, led by Lt Col Robert C. Olds, at Langley Field in Virginia.

Meanwhile, in Germany, as a result of von Richthofen's pressing, under great secrecy detailed drawings had been completed by July 1937 for a new liquid rocket-powered aircraft to be built by the Heinkel-Werke which was to be used purely as a rocket test aircraft. In conformity with earlier decisions, design and construction was isolated from all other company activity at Rostock-Marienehe.

The first prototype of an intended run of four test aircraft was built in early 1937, and it was to be fitted with a rocket engine provided by the HWA with the type designation R 102 (renamed R II 102 from September 1938) and fueled by a combination of alcohol and liquid oxygen. The aircraft was tested in the large wind tunnel at the Aerodynamische Versuchsanstalt at Göttingen in July 1938. The initial trials of what became the He 176 began sometime later, possibly in the late summer of 1938.

Some 29 flights had been made with Erich Warsitz at the controls by April 1939, during which the engine exhibited unstable thrust characteristics. Modifications to the engine and its control cured the problem, and the aircraft, again piloted by Warsitz, made a further 19 flights at Peenemünde and Rechlin between June 12 and November 8, 1939. On July 3 the aircraft had been demonstrated before Hitler, Göring, and the Generalluftzeugmeister, Ernst Udet, at Roggentin. Udet remained unimpressed, and all work on the He 176 was officially terminated by him on September 12, 1939.

Some nine months earlier in the USA, an experimental low-wing Y1B-17A monoplane – the 14th of its kind – was fitted with turbo-supercharged engines and delivered to the USAAC. Following successful trials, an order for 39 further such aircraft was placed under the designation B-17B, the "Y" prefix now having been dropped. Thus emerged the new "Flying Fortress."

But if America had its new long-range bomber, in 1939, in Britain too, designers at the Avro company under Roy Chadwick had been investigating the possibility of using four Rolls-Royce Merlin engines as replacements for the two Vulture units then in use in the Avro Manchester medium bomber. With such a revision, it was calculated that the new design would be capable of carrying a 12,000lb bombload over a distance of 1,000 miles or 8,000lbs over 1,600 miles at a speed of 245mph.

A series of design alterations ensued that saw new outer wing panels of increased span which incorporated the nacelles for the two new engines fitted to the Manchester's fuselage. The tail unit and center wing were also retained, and by November 15, 1940 it was decided to enter the new four-engined bomber into production as soon as existing commitments for the Manchester had been fulfilled. At this point as well, in view of the change in specification, it was felt to be beneficial to assign this "new" aircraft a new name, and thus Avro "Lancaster" was first used.

Unknown at the time, the enhanced design created at the Avro factory at Chadderton, near Oldham in Lancashire, and the work carried out by Boeing in Seattle, would establish the foundations of the Allied strategic bomber offensive against Germany that lay ahead. However, in Germany, other more ambitious aircraft designers had been at work to create an even more sophisticated rocket fighter, and one that within four years would engage the B-17 and the Lancaster in combat over the Third Reich, heralding a radical new form of aerial warfare.

CHRONOLOGY

1894
November 1 Alexander Lippisch, the originator of the Me 163, born in Munich.

1928
June Alexander Lippisch and Fritz Stamer conduct tests with tailless, rocket-powered models at the Wasserkuppe.

1935
July 28 Boeing Model 299 makes maiden flight at Seattle.

1937
January First Y1B-17 "Flying Fortress" delivered to Wright Field.

1939
July 3 He 176 lightweight rocket aircraft demonstrated for Hitler at Roggentin.

October Tests commence with the DFS 194 at Peenemünde.

1941
August 13 Heini Dittmar makes first powered take-off in Me 163A.

September First deliveries of B-17E to the US Army Air Force (USAAF).

1942
April Orders issued for establishment of *Erprobungskommando* (E.Kdo) 16 to test Me 163A and B.

July 1 First B-17 of VIII Bomber Command lands in England.

In the fall of 1943, the USAAF's Eighth Air Force intensified its daylight bombing offensive against Germany. Here, B-17F 42-3352 *VIRGIN'S DELIGHT* from the 410th BS/94th BG passes over the Rhine and the Focke-Wulf assembly plant at Marienburg during its bombing run on October 9, 1943. Flying Fortresses dropped gasoline incendiary bombs for the first time on this mission. Note the factory airfield runway to the left of the smoke generated by the burning plant. (Author's Collection)

July	Prototype Me 163 V2 fitted with two 20mm MG 151 cannon at Regensburg.
August 17	First raid by USAAF heavy bombers against Continental target made when 12 B-17s of the 97th Bombardment Group (BG) attack marshaling yards at Rouen. No casualties amongst the bomber crews.
September	Me 163A V4 cleared for powered flight at Peenemünde.

1943

September	B-17G reaches Eighth Air Force units in England, the aircraft being fitted with chin turret for defense against Luftwaffe head-on attacks and enclosed waist gun positions.
September	Commencement of training for first 21 pilots for Me 163 at Bad Zwischenahn. Includes towed (non-powered) flights.
October 14	USAAF attacks Schweinfurt with 229 B-17s, of which 60 are lost, 17 seriously damaged, and 121 damaged but repairable.

1944

February	At the beginning of February, E.Kdo 16 report five Me 163Bs with engines on strength, although at most only one or two are flight-capable.
March	First Me 163Bs used to form 1./JG 400 under the command of Hauptmann Robert Olejnik, which is transferred to Wittmundhafen on the 1st of the month.
April 19	Gen Dwight D. Eisenhower, Supreme Allied Commander in Europe, orders commencement of bombing offensive against German oil production plants.
July 19	In one of the very first encounters between the Me 163 and Allied aircraft, Unteroffizier Kurt Schiebeler in Me 163B V50 attempts, unsuccessfully, to intercept a P-38 Lightning.
July 28	1./JG 400, flying from Brandis, is involved in the first of six major engagements with USAAF heavy bombers, and their fighter escorts. On this occasion, 766 B-17Gs from the 1st and 3rd Bombardment Wings, escorted by P-38s and P-51s from 14 fighter groups, are targeting industrial sites in Merseburg-Leuna and Leipzig-Taucha. The USAAF INTOPS summary for the mission notes that "six to eight jet-propelled Me 163s were in the target area."

Rocket power – a technician makes last-minute checks as the HWK 109-509 A-1 motor of an Me 163B blasts a cloud of vaporized propellant from its rear vent in preparation for making a sharp take-off. [EN Archive]

DESIGN AND DEVELOPMENT

B-17 FLYING FORTRESS

With the appearance of the Y1B-17, American air power had reached a zenith – the United States had an aircraft that could wage war on the cities of other nations.

Following the USAAC tender issued on August 8, 1934, as mentioned in the Introduction, under the management of Idaho-born Edward Curtis Wells, a senior company engineer, Boeing injected everything it had into the process, committing almost all of its available capital and labor force. This saw the company enhance the design of its Model 247 all-metal commercial airliner and incorporate elements of the Model 294 bomber, including four engines.

A very streamlined design eventually emerged that could carry a crew of eight comprising a pilot, co-pilot, bombardier, navigator/radio operator, and four gunners. The weapons for the latter would be housed at four blister-type flexible machine gun stations in a dorsal position in the fuselage just above the wing trailing edge, in a ventral fuselage position just behind the wing trailing edge, and on either side of the rear fuselage in a waist position, each of which would accommodate a 0.30-cal. or 0.50-cal machine gun.

Construction of the Model 299 began on August 16, 1934, and the prototype took to the air from Seattle on July 28, 1935 with Boeing test pilot Leslie Tower at the controls. It was submitted to the USAAC as the Model X-299, but the army objected to the designation as being too similar to its experimental military project numbers, so it was officially changed to B-299. Following an impressive, record-breaking flight from Seattle to the USAAC's testing facility at Wright Field, the test program seemed to progress quite well. The Model 299 showed promise over the competing designs submitted by Martin and Douglas, and exceeded all USAAC requirements in terms of speed, climb, range, and bombload. Subsequently, the USAAC arranged to purchase 65 test machines under the designation Y1B-17. It was a large machine, with each of its mainwheels being almost as tall as a man.

Following the crash on October 30, 1935 which inflicted mortal injuries on Tower and Hill, it was discovered that elevator locks had not been removed prior to flight. The accident almost rang the death knell for the Model 299 (B-299), and was grist to the mill for those who opposed the prospects of a vast fleet of "strategic" bombers, for they questioned their cost and likely effectiveness. Others believed a four-engined aircraft like the B-299 was simply too much for one, or even two pilots to control. The USAAC canceled any further production, with the tender award being switched to Douglas for the cheaper, but less sophisticated B-18.

However, in January 1936, in an apparent about-turn, the USAAC placed an order for 13 new test models under the designation Y1B-17, and these were to be assigned to the 2nd BG under the command of Lt Col Robert C. Olds at Langley Field. Key changes to the design saw the Y1B-17 fitted with four 930hp Wright R-1820-39 Cyclone engines in place of the Model 299's 750hp Pratt & Whitney R-1690 Hornets. Again disaster was to strike when, on December 2, 1936, the first such machine careered along the runway at Boeing Field for 80 yards following a brake failure and skidded to an ignoble stop in the midst of a Congressional investigation. Doubts grew. Oblivion loomed.

Fortunately, the first Y1B-17 was delivered to the 2nd BG in March 1937, with a further 11 being phased in up to August 4 that year, and the 13th aircraft going to Wright Field. This would be a critical time in the government's, the USAAC's, and the public's perception of the aircraft, since the 2nd BG crews – who formed the USAAC's total heavy bomber strength – were charged with conducting a thorough assessment of the aircraft's strengths and weaknesses. "We knew if a YB crashed," recalled the 2nd BG's then 2Lt Robert F. Travis, "we could probably say goodbye to the nation's bomber program."

Fortunately, 1938 saw a series of spectacular publicity and record-breaking flights flown by the 2nd BG. Lt Col Olds achieved an east-to-west transcontinental record of 12hrs 50min, before immediately turning around and breaking the west-to-east

The Model 299 prototype was photographed at Boeing Field shortly after it was rolled out in July 1935. Note the early nose configuration. The aircraft flew for the first time on July 28, 1935 and was destroyed at Wright Field on October 30 that same year. (USAF)

An early B-17D photographed at Wright Field. Powered by four 1,200hp Wright R-1820-65 turbo-supercharged radials, it was the last model to feature the small "shark fin" tail and an underside "bathtub" turret. It was armed with one 0.30-cal. and six 0.50-cal. machine guns and could carry 4,800lbs of bombs over a range of 3,400 miles. (USAF)

record, averaging 245mph in 10hrs 46min. Other promotional flights were made as far afield as Argentina. The YBs so far commissioned flew for more than 9,000 hours over a distance of 1,800,000 miles without any serious accident or damage.

Meanwhile, in January 1939, a 14th and experimental aircraft, designated the Y1B-17A, was fitted with turbo-supercharged engines and delivered to the USAAC. Following successful trials, which demonstrated that its ceiling had increased by 9,000ft and top speed by 30mph at 25,000ft, an order for 39 further such aircraft was placed under the designation B-17B. Examples began to reach the USAAC in 1939, equipping the 2nd and 7th BGs. Both groups subsequently conducted high-altitude precision bombing trials in California, with ostensibly encouraging results, albeit in near perfect conditions.

The B-17B benefited from being powered by four 1,200hp nine-cylinder Wright R-1820-G205A engines, and in the B-17C which followed, the removal of the gun blisters gave the four gunners more workable positions with greater flexibility and field-of-fire. The B-17D, with a wingspan just short of 104ft, saw both internal and external refinements, including improved electrical systems, and further gun stations in dorsal (aft of the cockpit), and "bathtub" turrets. Overall, the armament increased to an array of one 0.30-cal. and six 0.50-cal. machine guns, the aircraft also incorporating more "fortress"-like armor protection, while externally, engine cooling was enhanced and external bomb racks removed.

The B and C variants saw use in the Philippines, Hawaii, and with the Royal Air Force (RAF) in Britain. However, operating the aircraft as the Fortress I, and fitted with self-sealing fuel tanks, the RAF failed to be impressed by the Boeing as a potential daylight bomber. One machine, which had been attacked by German fighters over Brest, in France, on July 24, 1941, effectively disintegrated on landing, while a little over two weeks earlier, Fortress Is on a raid to Wilhelmshaven were unable to defend themselves because their guns froze at altitude. Furthermore, they missed the target.

There was exasperation on the part of the Americans. One USAAC officer recalled:

I was in England when the planes arrived. We explained to the British our doctrine for their use. We told them that the crews had to be well trained, that a crew should drop 200 practice bombs before attacking a real target, that the planes were designed to fly in formation for protective purposes and that by using them as trainers, trained crews could be ready to operate the new, properly equipped Fortresses when we delivered them. For some reason, which only the British understand, they decided to immediately use the planes offensively.

In September 1941 Boeing introduced the B-17E. Six feet longer than the C-model and seven tons heavier than the original Model 299, it boasted a substantially redesigned airframe which featured an increase in the size of the horizontal and vertical tail sections intended to offer the improved aerodynamic qualities necessary to provide a reliable bomber. It also had a tail gun position – a "stinger" – for added defense in the rear hemisphere. The dorsal turret was powered and the ventral turret beneath the center fuselage section aft of the bomb-bay was remotely-controlled and fitted with a periscope, resulting in a formidable total of eight 0.50-cal. machine guns, with a single 0.30-cal gun mounted in a Plexiglas nose. Writing in *The Aeroplane* in February 1944, one British journalist described a novel feature of the B-17E:

> As the aeroplane is suitable for aromatic fuel, the crew members may smoke while in the air, and so the navigator/bomb-aimer is supplied with a built-in ash-tray and cigarette receptacle.

Nevertheless, the bomb-bay in the B-17E was appreciably smaller than that of the British Stirling, Halifax, and Lancaster "heavy" bombers of the time. The bomb-bay doors of the B-17 were approximately 11ft in length, whereas those of the Lancaster were 33ft. RAF technical officers remained skeptical over the operational capabilities of the new American Fortress I. Firstly, they felt that its defensive armament was too weak to offer sufficient protection, and the much-vaunted tail gun was too cramped, while the ventral ball turret was considered so awkward as to be useless. Furthermore, the 4,000lb "Blockbuster" bombs used by the RAF could not be accommodated in the bomb-bay, and normal bombloads were too small unless the fuselage fuel tanks were removed, which, of course, compromised range.

By the time the Japanese attacked Pearl Harbor on December 7, 1941, the USAAF had 150 B-17s on strength – the fruits of an efficient production "co-operative" of Boeing (who supplied the drawings and tooling), the Douglas Aircraft Company, and the Vega Aircraft Company, a subsidiary of Lockheed. Together, they would build the B-17F, which featured several internal refinements. For example, while the forward and downward vision through the bow window of the B-17E was excellent, the view

Smiling crewmen of one of the first B-17s to arrive in England hitch rides on ammunition and bomb trailers out to their aircraft. The officer in the foreground straddles a 2,000lb bomb. The men are clad in leather flying gear and life vests. (Author's Collection)

through the single-piece Plexiglas nose cap of the B-17F was even better. The new nose was longer and deeper, and contributed to improved performance in the air.

On January 2, 1942, Maj Gen Henry "Hap" Arnold, Commanding General of the USAAF, signed the order activating the Eighth Air Force, with VIII Bomber Command being established six days later under the leadership of Brig Gen Ira C. Eaker. In August, the first B-17s flew to England via the North Atlantic ferry route, having staged via Labrador, Greenland, and Prestwick, in Scotland, equipping the recently-formed 97th and 301st BGs at bases in Hertfordshire and Northamptonshire (the aircraft of the 92nd BG flew directly from Newfoundland to Scotland, covering a distance of 2,120 miles). For the crews – despite being pitifully ill-trained on the Flying Fortress, its radio equipment, and armament, and quartered a long way from home – it was akin to the start of a great adventure. By the end of August, a total of 119 B-17s were in England.

It was not long before the first B-17s were "blooded." During the late afternoon of August 17, 12 Flying Fortresses of the 97th BG, escorted by four squadrons of Spitfire IXs from the RAF, bombed the marshaling yards at Sotteville, near Rouen in occupied France, dropping 18 tons of bombs. "Going along for the ride" as an observer was Brig Gen Eaker. Fw 190s of II./JG 26 (whose pilots wrongly identified the bombers as British Stirlings) and JG 2 launched an attack over Ypreville. Two B-17s were lightly damaged by Flak, but there were no casualties. An encouraging new dimension had opened in the air war over Europe, although Eaker quickly commented "One swallow doesn't make a summer" after receiving a note of congratulations from Air Marshal Sir Arthur Harris of RAF Bomber Command.

That winter, Peter Masefield, the bespectacled Technical Editor of the British periodical *The Aeroplane*, visited the 97th BG at Grafton Underwood, in Northamptonshire, and was invited to board B-17E *Yankee Doodle*. Actually an aircraft of the 92nd BG but assigned to the former group, it had taken part in the Sotteville mission. Masefield recorded what he saw for his readers:

Long, low, sleek, battle-scarred – a brown shape against the grey of the English Winter's afternoon. The interior of the Fortress is divided into seven compartments. Beginning at the rear, there is first of all the hand-operated tail gun position under the rudder. Next comes the compartment in which the retracted tail wheel is housed, and then the main rear cabin with the two waist guns at the side and the top of the "ball turret" in the floor, just behind the cabin's forward bulkhead. In front of the bulkhead is the radio

Having cycled to the edge of the runway at Grafton Underwood, and in what is probably a posed photograph, groundcrew wave at a B-17E of the 97th BG as it lifts into the air in the summer of 1942. The bomber still carries its pre-war identification markings on the underside of the wings. (Author's Collection)

compartment with a 0.50-inch machine gun in the roof, and then a narrow catwalk leads through the middle of the bomb-bay to the underneath of the top turret. Immediately in front of the turret is the pilot's cabin, with dual controls and seats side-by-side. Between the two pilots, a little alleyway drops down and leads forward to the extreme nose, with its accommodation for navigator, bomb aimer, and front gunner.

Apparently impressed, Masefield prophesized:

No American-manned Fortress has flown over Germany, but when the time does come, the height and speed of the Fortress formations should enable them to show up against that opposition at least as well as any other aeroplane of their size now flying.

Indeed, Eaker was already clear as to how his bombers would target the enemy, as he noted in the summer of 1942:

First the factories, sheds, docks, and ports in which the enemy builds his submarines and from which he launches his submarine efforts. Next, his aircraft factories and other key munitions-manufacturing establishments. Third, his lines of communication. A subsidiary purpose of our early bombing operations will be to determine our capacity to destroy pinpoint targets by daylight precision bombing and our ability to beat off fighter opposition.

In conclusion, however, in his assessment of the Flying Fortress, Peter Masefield wrote:

The question remains – are the defenses of industrial Germany such that daylight bombing in force in good weather will result in uneconomic casualties? We may soon know the answer.

That answer would come – with startling decisiveness – in the months ahead.

Me 163

In the autumn of 1937, Dr.-Ing. Hermann Lorenz, a *Gruppenleiter* (section leader) within the RLM's LC 1 department (aircraft research), together with his assistant, Fliegerstabsing Dr. Jenissen, visited the workshops of the *Deutsche Forschungsanstalt für Segelflug* (DFS) based at Griesheim to the west of Darmstadt. They had gone there to meet with Alexander Lippisch, a 43-year-old glider and light aircraft designer of some repute who had been working on a series of experimental tailless aircraft known as the *Delta* series. Lippisch was an enthusiastic man, perhaps even impulsive, but he was also determined and uncompromising in his beliefs, and thus, on occasion, was not the easiest of people to work with.

Lippisch and Lorenz did not enjoy a particularly harmonious relationship, with the latter disapproving of the former's hasty and sometimes rash style of getting things done. Such methods were at odds with the pedestrian processes of the RLM.

Crouching on one knee, Alexander Lippisch, the glider and light aircraft designer who would go on to design and create the Me 163, appears to ponder a wooden model of one of his Delta series as it sits on a launch rail in 1934. (Ransom Collection)

The progressive concept and design of the *Delta* series had both raised eyebrows and generated considerable interest among the aeronautical fraternity. But Lippisch's work was not that of a fanciful man, for he had been deeply interested in the science of flight since having been inspired by Orville Wright's flights at Tempelhof, in Berlin, in September 1909.

Lippisch had experienced World War I as an aerial reconnaissance interpreter on the Eastern Front, and after the conflict he had joined the Zeppelin Works and then Dornier as an aerodynamicist. Following a failed attempt to carry out aerial mapping for the Brazilian government, he found employment for his services as an aerodynamicist with a small aircraft company on the Wasserkuppe in 1921. There, at the cradle of German gliding development and in the shadow of the restrictions of the Treaty of Versailles imposed upon Germany, he also became involved with Gottlob Espenlaub, an entrepreneurial former carpenter who also designed and built gliders and who, in late 1929, had conducted experiments with a rocket-powered aircraft of his own design while earning a living by making furniture and repairing aircraft.

Lippisch and Espenlaub were both beguiled by the notion of tailless aircraft, and in this regard it is believed that they had drawn their influences from Friedrich Wenk, another 'amateur' Wasserkuppe aviator who, in 1921, had designed his own version of a gull-winged, tailless glider. Thus inspired, Lippisch and Espenlaub developed the Espenlaub E 2, but enthusiasm for the project took a dent when all Espenlaub's attempts to fly the craft ended in stalls and crashes.

In 1931 the first in the *Delta* series, the *Delta I*, was demonstrated at Berlin-Adlershof fitted with a pusher propeller-driven engine, and this served to raise wider interest in the prospect of tailless aircraft. However, according to Lippisch:

> My demands for extensive support to conduct the necessary basic research and funding
> for tests and personnel were refused by government authorities. It was then very clear to
> me that it was important to establish a scientific basis for the design of this type of aircraft
> and, after the previous pioneering work, to investigate systematically the various problems
> that had arisen. Because these new ideas were based on rudimentary scientific data,
> however, their inclusion in current aircraft design practice was hindered at a time when
> it might have been possible to increase the lead already gained in their development.

Undaunted, however, and driven by his uncompromising nature, Lippisch pressed on with developing the *Delta* series. The ensuing low, cantilever-winged *Delta III* and *IV*, fitted with tractor propellers, suffered from instability problems. Another designer, Gerhard Fieseler, had wanted to fly a *Delta* in the 1932 *Europa-Rundflug* after Lippisch had spoken enthusiastically about tailless designs. Fieseler queried the issue of stability, or the lack of it, at which Lippisch apparently stated, "I'm prepared to put my head over the parapet." Although Lippisch prepared the *Delta IV* accordingly for Fieseler, and fitted it with two British 75hp Pobjoy engines installed in the nose and tail, respectively, it was not ready enough.

"The aircraft was also to have a small wingspan, folding wings and," wrote Lippisch, "to improve lift during take-off, auxiliary canards behind the front engine and above the wing center-section. I had begged Fieseler not to test fly the bird, but to let us know by telephone when it was ready, and [test pilot, Günther] Groenhoff and I would then go to [Fieseler] Kassel. I called Groenhoff because the first *Delta IV* had only just been ready to fly when Fieseler jammed himself into the cockpit and slammed open the throttle. He did not tell us what happened after that, but the aircraft was quite smashed up." "Badly designed," Fieseler remarked somewhat unfairly following his mishap. "We must start from scratch again."

Lippisch admitted in his memoirs that the aircraft "had practically every bad quality one could think of," and further crashes followed. Indeed, increasingly, Lippisch's designs were considered difficult to fly. Thus, by 1933, officially at least, work on the *Delta* series ceased. But behind the scenes Lippisch continued development of the *Delta IV* at Griesheim, convinced that there was a place for tailless aircraft. Having managed to get the machine back from Fieseler, Lippisch set about rebuilding it without its canard surfaces and pusher engine. This revision became the *Delta IVa*, but it crashed again when test pilot Erich Wiegmeyer endeavored to avoid a mid-air collision with a Klemm towplane.

The *Delta IVb* and *IVc* followed, and they incorporated various modifications to the wing. On January 9, 1937, the renowned and experienced competition pilot Flugkapitän Heinrich "Heini" Dittmar took to the air in the *Delta IVc* from Griesheim. Dittmar had won the 1932 and 1933 Rhön gliding competitions, and in February 1934 he achieved a world altitude record for gliders when he reached 4,675m while in South America. Later that year he broke the world distance record for gliders (375km) and the altitude record for two-seat gliders (2,700m). In 1935 Dittmar was the first pilot to cross the Alps. For his part, he had few complaints about the *Delta IVc* with its distinctive, downward inclining wingtips.

Then, in 1937, Lippisch commenced investigating, on a practical level, the effects of comparative fuselage designs on tailless aircraft. Two test designs resulted from this – the DFS 40 was, in effect, an innovative, if somewhat ungainly, flying wing in which the pilot and the engine were contained within the profile of the wing, while the DFS 194, created as a result of a 1935 contract from the RLM, was a mid-wing design featuring a stubby fuselage. It was originally intended that power was to come from an Argus AS 10c engine driving a pusher propeller. By the time both types commenced testing, they remained without engines.

Gottlob Espenlaub, center, stands in the trailing edge curve of his first tailless aircraft, a hang glider which he co-designed with Alexander Lippisch, also seen here in the foreground, in a photograph from the 1920s. (Ransom Collection)

When Lorenz and Jenissen arrived at Griesheim in 1937, Lippisch showed the RLM representatives around his workshop, in which was parked the *Delta IVc* (known officially by this time as the DFS 39) and the new DFS 194. When asked which of the two aircraft had the better flight-handling qualities, Lippisch responded that it was the DFS 39, to which Lorenz then enquired whether a second such aircraft could be built, but with a different fuselage? Lorenz then explained that the RLM wanted to test a new engine which would need to be installed in the rear of the fuselage, and so the cockpit had to be located forward, unlike the present location in the DFS 39. Lippisch recalled "replying drily: 'You want to try out a new rocket engine?'" Lorenz was furious at the mention of this, and ordered Lippisch to never mention the word "rocket" publicly again.

However, with a contract from the RLM, and once briefed further in Berlin, under the furtive codename "Project X," Lippisch set about working out the aerodynamic qualities of such an aircraft that would be powered by a liquid-fueled engine giving 400kg thrust. The DFS was also to build the wing in its workshop.

Meanwhile, in 1935, former marine engineer Hellmuth Walter, with government assistance, established his own company, the Hellmuth Walter Kommanditgesellschaft (HWK), in the Baltic seaport of Kiel. His aim was to develop a power system that utilized the energy contained in concentrated hydrogen peroxide, an oxygen-rich liquid, for military purposes. As part of his work, in 1936, Walter began developing rocket motors that used liquid propellant as a means of aircraft take-off assistance, as well as *Z-Stoff* ("cold") and a *C-Stoff/ T-Stoff* oxidizer/fuel combination ("hot") engines for aircraft propulsion. With this level of work underway, HWK was awarded a contract by the RLM to produce a controllable rocket motor using hydrogen peroxide as the main element of its fuel. *T-Stoff* was a highly concentrated 80 percent solution of hydrogen peroxide.

In terms of *T-Stoff*, Walter maintained that the compound was non-detonable by impact or shock, but such concentrations are liable to decompose violently in the presence of impurities such as dust, rust, metallic particles, and organic matter. Hydrogen peroxide also decomposes rapidly when it comes into contact with one of a wide variety of catalysts including calcium or sodium permanganate. With rapid decomposition, the energy release is similar to that of gunpowder, and hence a superheated steam and oxygen propellant results in a process known as a "cold" motor. When *T-* and *C-Stoff* came together they exploded spontaneously and violently.

C-Stoff consisted of 30 percent hydrazine hydrate and 57 percent methyl alcohol, but the

The Lippisch *Delta IVc* (DFS 39), coded D-ENFL, turns low over the treeline at Griesheim with Flugkapitän Heinrich "Heini" Dittmar at the controls. The aircraft first took to the air in January 1937. (Ransom Collection)

heat caused by this combination would raise the temperature in a combustion chamber to more than 1,850 degrees, so it was diluted with 13 percent water. This lowered the temperature to 1,750 degrees, with the difference in temperatures between this and a decomposition engine resulting in what was referred to as a "hot" motor.

Hydrazine hydrate is a powerful reducing agent, and it ignited spontaneously when mixed with *T-Stoff*. There was, however, a delay in the self-igniting process that would have allowed sufficient time for an explosive amount of liquid to accumulate in a combustion chamber. In order to accelerate the reaction and prevent this problem, a catalyst was added to the *C-Stoff* in the form of potassium cuprocyanide in a concentration of 0.6gm per liter.

HWK carried out extensive research to establish the correct dilutions and proportions to make *T-Stoff* powerful enough to use as a motor propellant, stable enough for storage, and controllable during decomposition.

In early 1939, based on the progress of their respective tasks, the RLM transferred the overseeing of Lippisch's and HWK's contracts from its LC 1 research department to LC 2, its aircraft development section. The management of the contracts was assigned to Flugbaumeister Dipl.-Ing. Hans-Martin Antz, together with engine specialist Helmut Schelp from LC 3.

By then it had been realized that such was the level of the development task, and its complexities, that they were beyond the capabilities of the DFS at Griesheim, and so "Project X," along with Lippisch and an initial group of 12 of his key colleagues, was transferred to the remit of the Messerschmitt company at Augsburg, in Bavaria – work commenced here on January 2, 1939. Eventually, more specialists from the DFS followed, and they were gathered under a new Department "L" (Lippisch) at Augsburg under the overall supervision of Lippisch, who remembered:

> The work did not get going very quickly. As it had been decided to increase the engine's thrust to 750kg at full power, the original design had had to be discarded and work on a new layout started. Everything except the engine was to be built by Messerschmitt, the fuselage and center-section of aluminum and the wings of wood. First, I tried to get detailed performance data about the engine, but no one really knew anything about it.

After being integrated within Messerschmitt, "Project X" was assigned the type name "Me 163" (a designation previously given to the canceled Bf 163 low-speed liaison and observation aircraft). The two diminutive DFS 194 prototypes thus far completed were subsumed into the project, the V1 being configured for the fitment of a Walter motor, while the V2 remained unaltered, and was flown by Dittmar as a glider to assess in-flight handling. This, despite the fact that Lippisch and his team remained largely uninformed on details of the planned rocket motor.

Upon the outbreak of war at the beginning of September 1939, work on the new Me 163 project was downgraded in priority, along with several other projects. Eventually, however, after the Generalluftzeugmeister, Ernst Udet, continued to show interest in it, the DFS 194 V1 was fitted with a "cold" HWK R I-203 300kg-thrust rocket motor at the *Erprobungsstelle* at Peenemünde-West. Lippisch recalled:

The DFS 194 under construction at Messerschmitt Augsburg in 1939. Although here it has no Walter rocket motor installed, for the first time, the future Me 163 can be seen emerging in the design. (Ransom Collection)

The first powered flights with the Walter rocket-propelled DFS 194 were made at Peenemünde in the summer of 1940. The results not only matched our expectations but also exceeded performance estimates. The aircraft's configuration, as well as the method of flight-testing using towed and gliding flights, proved very satisfactory. This experience stood the '163 in good stead, and it was able to be immediately included in its design.

Significantly, the craft attained a maximum speed of 550km/h, exceeding that of Heinkel's Walter rocket-powered He 176, and it achieved an astonishingly high rate-of-climb to 3,000m.

After suffering hold-ups to progress in the first half of 1941 due to conflicts between the former DFS team's expectations and Messerschmitt's production methods, as well as a six-month delay in delivery of the Walter motor, finally the V4 (the fourth prototype in the new Me 163A series), coded KE+SW, arrived at Peenemünde-West, having been air-towed in glider form from Augsburg. It was then fitted with a 750kg thrust Walter R II 203 "cold" engine and a jettisonable undercarriage dolly. On August 13, 1941, Heini Dittmar left the ground to take the V4 up on its first powered take-off. The little aircraft made an impressive sight as it streaked upwards with a blast of rocket effluent trailing behind it. Lippisch wrote:

> Our success in 1941 was crowned by Heini flying faster than 1,000km/h. At just over 1,000km/h the shock wave caused the airflow over the outer wing to separate suddenly and the aircraft pitched nose down, the instruments registering a negative acceleration of 11g. Heini pulled the throttle back quickly, the aircraft slowed down and he was able to take control again. In the evening, the Askania theodolite measurements were evaluated: the final result revealed a speed of 1,003km/h!'

It was to be the dawn of the Luftwaffe's new operational rocket interceptor.

TECHNICAL
SPECIFICATIONS

B-17F/G FLYING FORTRESS

The Eighth Air Force launched its bomber war against Nazi Germany with the B-17E. This magnificent and quite majestic four-engined aircraft came off the production line in September 1941 and arrived in England in July 1942. Seven tons heavier and 40 percent faster than Boeing's original Model 299, it represented an extensive redesign and improvement over the earlier C- and D-models, with a major aerodynamic reworking of the tail section and rear fuselage areas in order to improve stability for bombing. Most evident was the distinctive, low, sweeping fillet that pulled back from about halfway along the fuselage as part of an extended and more elegant tail assembly.

The fuselage of the B-17 was formed from an all-metal, semi-monocoque structure, constructed of Alclad fastened with alloy rivets, and within which was built a number of bulkheads separating four sections. These comprised the forward section housing the bombardier-navigator and pilots' compartments, the center section containing the bomb-bay, the rear fuselage section, and the tail section. Internally, there was a maximum cross-section height of 103in. and a maximum width of 90in.

The USAAF's first truly combat-ready version of the Flying Fortress, refined following experience in the Pacific and from early operations conducted from Britain with the RAF (which had used the D and E variants as the Fortress I and II, respectively) and the Eighth Air Force, the B-17F actually differed very little from its

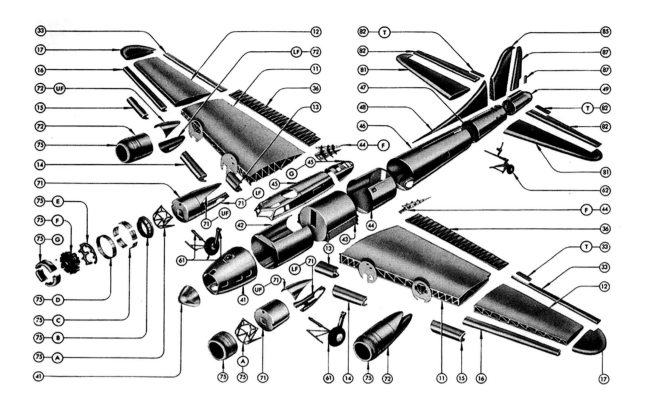

A schematic diagram from the 1944 Field Service Manual issued by Boeing in Seattle for the "Model B-17G Bombardment Airplane – The Flying Fortress." The diagram shows the complete sub-assembly breakdown. According to the manual, "Disassembling the fuselage, except at stations 1, 6, or 11, is a major operation. The nacelles and their fairings are also difficult to remove from the wing, and should be taken off only when absolutely necessary." (Author Collection)

predecessor, the E-model. The main distinguishing external feature was a new frameless nose cone.

Internally, however, no fewer than 400 minor changes were undertaken. These included re-engineering to the leading edge contours of the cowlings of the four 1,200hp Wright R-1820-97 radial engines to avoid the new Hamilton Standard "paddle blade" propellers striking them when feathered, as well as improvements to the oxygen system (which suffered from inadequate supply and freezing) landing gear and brakes. Enhancements were also made to the bomb racks and ball turret (the least favored position in the aircraft, where excess ice and oil played havoc with the guns), and an automatic pilot/bombsight link was added. With field additions made in Britain, the B-17F could carry 12 or 13 0.50-cal. Browning M2 machine guns, making it the most heavily armed bomber in service.

The aircraft was operated "officially" by a crew of ten – pilot, co-pilot, navigator and bombardier (all officers), and flight engineer/top turret gunner, radio operator/roof hatch gunner, two waist gunners, ball turret gunner, and tail gunner (all NCOs).

The first F-models were delivered by Boeing Seattle in late May 1942, with Douglas at Long Beach and Lockheed-Vega following during the summer. By the late summer of 1943, all three plants accounted for an average output of 400 aircraft per month.

In terms of armament, the lessons learned in the Pacific prompted the fitting of a 0.50-cal. Browning in each of two newly created Plexiglas observation windows either side of the nose, to be used by the bombardier or the navigator. These additions meant that the B-17F carried 12 or 13 machine guns. However, not all machines benefited

B-17G ARMAMENT FIELDS-OF-FIRE

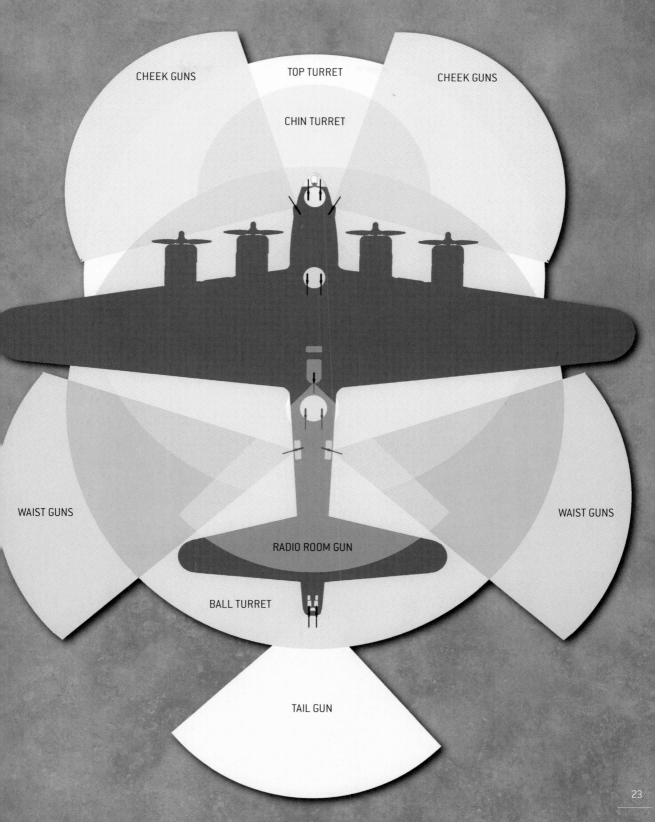

CHEEK GUNS

TOP TURRET

CHEEK GUNS

CHIN TURRET

WAIST GUNS

WAIST GUNS

RADIO ROOM GUN

BALL TURRET

TAIL GUN

from this modification, and many soldiered on in early 1943 with the nose adapted to accommodate a single 0.50-cal. gun, with a mounting able to absorb the increased recoil.

Engineers of the 97th BG devised a field modification whereby the 40 minutes it took to hand-crank a full load of ordnance into the bomb-bay was halved.

The B-17G was the last production model of the Flying Fortress, with first examples being delivered to the USAAF from September 1943. The Eighth Air Force deployed it on operations from the following month, and it took part in the second Schweinfurt raid alongside B-17Fs. Effectively an organic development of the F-model, the B-17G is perhaps best identified by its Bendix "chin" turret, which was fitted with twin 0.50-cal. Brownings with 365 rounds per gun, and intended as an antidote to head-on attacks by Luftwaffe fighters.

The B-17G featured a frameless Plexiglas nose cone, below which was fitted a twin-gun Bendix "chin" turret which was positioned immediately beneath the bombardier's seat on a pivot housing for the lateral rotation of the turret. The remote control for operating the turret and its 0.50-cal. Brownings was mounted on a tubular bracket, which could be clipped away to starboard and swung quickly into a central position for operation. The twin hand grips – known as "dead man's handles" – had small inserts which, when depressed, made an electrical contact in the turret operation circuit. The handle's movement controlled the relative movement of both turret and guns, as well as the reflector sight in the upper section of the nose cone. (Author's Collection)

With a wingspan of 103ft 9.4in. and tail span of 43ft, the B-17G had a wing area of 1,420sq ft, while the tail, fin, and rudder area was 331.1 sq. ft. The aircraft was 74ft 3.9in. in length, 24ft 6.91in. in height with tail up, and it had an undercarriage track of 21ft 1.52in.

Powered by the same Wright engines as the F-model, the B-17G could carry 2,810 US gallons of fuel in its wing tanks, with provision for two overload tanks in the bomb-bay accommodating another 820 US gallons. It weighed 36,135lbs empty and on take-off, its maximum permissible weight was 65,500lbs.

The fuselage was divided into seven sections from the nose running aft. Firstly, 1) the bombardier's and navigator's compartment with a rear hatchway leading above to 2) the pilot's cabin, behind the seats of which were oxygen bottles and the upper gun turret, then 3) the bomb-bay, with stowage for life-rafts and a cat-walk between the bomb racks to 4) the radio compartment, then 5) the main rear cabin containing the ball turret, emergency flotation radio set and aerial kite, waist gun mountings and the main entry door on the starboard side aft, then 6) the housing for the retractable tail wheel and automatic pilot stabilizer and 7) tail turret beneath the rudder.

The G-model could carry a normal maximum load of six 1,600lb bombs and two 4,000lb bombs. Maximum speed was 287mph at 25,000ft or 302mph at 25,000ft under "war emergency" power. Cruising speed was 182mph at 10,000ft. Range with a 6,000lb bombload at 10,000ft was 2,000 miles at 182mph.

First introduced on some of the last B-17Fs, the Bendix chin turret was designed to be operated under remote control by the bombardier, but its installation forced the removal of the direction-finding loop originally housed in a streamlined fairing. This equipment was re-installed just forward of the bomb-bay and a little to the left of the fuselage centerline.

In the winter of 1943–44, the Sperry upper turret was replaced by a Bendix type twin 0.50-cal. with 375 rounds per gun which offered improved visibility and control, although they were prone to fires which broke out as a result of frayed electrical wiring and oxygen lines. The earlier design of the tail turret, which featured a tunnel opening at the very end of the fuselage, was changed for a new Cheyenne (named after the town in Wyoming where it had been designed at the United Air Lines Modification Center) twin 0.50-cal. turret. The latter had larger windows that gave better visibility, a greater field-of-fire and a reflector sight for the tail gunner, each gun being armed with 500 rounds. This was a significant improvement over the former turret's 30-degree traverse and comparatively primitive ring-and-bead sight positioned outside and beyond the much smaller gunner's window. The twin 0.50-cal. weapons were moved nearer the gunner, and the mounting was protected by a semi-circular cover.

In its usual form, the B-17G brandished no fewer than 13 0.50-cal. Browning M2 machine guns, two each in chin, upper, ball (500 rounds per gun), and tail turrets, with further such weapons in the nose cheek positions (610 rounds in total) and waist windows (600 rounds per gun). The weapons in the latter positions were mounted in open windows on operational missions, subjecting the gunners to the icy blast of slipstream. Another problem was that the two waist gunners, clad in their bulky flying gear, would often bump into each other, posing the risk of unintentionally pulling out an oxygen connection. Eventually, Plexiglas coverings were fitted. The radio room gun position was also open during missions, and a similar solution had to be introduced there as well.

A *Flight* magazine journalist who inspected the B-17G summarized:

> The Flying Fortress is now, after its nine years of development, a very good military aircraft, well-liked by its crews, sturdy of build, and eminently capable of both taking and handing out great punishment.

Me 163

After Heini Dittmar's flight in the Me 163 V4 on August 13, 1941, trials with the Me 163A continued, with only very limited activity throughout the remainder of 1941 and through to the summer of 1942. A second A-model, V5 Wk-Nr 163000002, coded GG+EA, was cleared for unpowered flight at Augsburg on November 8, 1941, and it made two flights the same day with Dittmar at the controls. This aircraft remained at Augsburg for at least a few days before being transferred north to Peenemünde to join the V4. Three further prototypes, the V6–V8, would trickle into readiness during the late spring and summer of 1942.

A second test pilot, Leutnant Rudolf "Rudi" Opitz, had joined the test program. He was another highly qualified glider pilot and instructor from the Wasserkuppe, and his activity as an instructor at the DFS in Darmstadt meant that he was familiar with Lippisch and his work. In May 1940 Opitz had flown DFS 230 gliders during the airborne assaults on Fort Eben Emael and the bridges over the Albert Canal, in Belgium. In August 1941 he was posted to Department "L" at Augsburg, for whom he was sent to Peenemünde as a test pilot for the Me 163 development program on behalf of the *Erprobungsstelle* there.

Sometime in August 1942 at Peenemünde, Dittmar briefed Opitz on the Me 163A (the V4), and Opitz was confident enough to immediately attempt a "sharp start" (powered take-off). In this he was hampered by what he described as ground waves (radio waves propagating parallel to and adjacent to the surface of the Earth), but very quickly he was airborne and out over the Baltic. Against guidance, he decided to retain the aircraft's take-off dolly rather than jettisoning it, and so after what was a trouble-free, but short, flight due to only a part fuel load, Opitz landed without damage. His landing distance was longer than normal, however, as a result of the lack of drag on the grass field arising from the dolly compared to the skid. Opitz later wrote:

> I was informed that the prior consensus of opinion about possibly landing with the take-off dolly still attached had been that a crash would be the likely result. I proved them wrong. Subsequently, all further Me 163 operations had the take-off runways scrutinized for the presence of ground waves in advance.

Meanwhile, in 1941, plans had been underway for the production of an armed, operational variant of the Me 163, the B-model, with output accelerated so that the first batch would be available in early 1942. Discussions between the RLM and Messerschmitt centered around an order for 70 aircraft to be built by the company at Obertraubling. At a meeting held at the RLM in Berlin on August 29, 1941, Theodor Croneiss, a board director of Messerschmitt, handed a description of the "enlarged version of the Me 163" to Flugbaumeister Antz. Despite a potentially competing, but not tailless, swept-back wing, pulse jet-powered fighter design produced by the Messerschmitt Project Office under Waldemar Voigt known as the P.1079, Professor Wilhelm "Willy" Messerschmitt had stressed that it was Lippisch and not Voigt who was to investigate *tailless* designs.

Thus, specific, detailed pre-production work on the Me 163B commenced on September 1, 1941, and shortly thereafter, a description of the aircraft, together with a proposal for production, was submitted to the RLM. Manufacturing of the first four series prototypes, the B V1–V4, was planned to start as early as October 1, with the first two aircraft at least to be built in Augsburg. The remaining 66 production Me 163Bs were to be constructed at the Messerschmitt plants at Regensburg and Obertraubling. However, various delays resulting from a lack of draughtsmen promised by the RLM, as well as a lack of aerodynamicists and a wind tunnel model, meant that initial preparations did not start until December 1941. There were further problems after that due to a shortage of construction materials and engines from the HWK.

Finally, on June 26, 1942, the first prototype Me 163B, V1 KE+SX, made its first unpowered towed flight from Augsburg, piloted by Dittmar.

As production falteringly progressed through 1942, and with BMW also failing to

Mechanics roll the jettisonable undercarriage dolly beneath the landing skid of an Me 163 for attachment. Once the dolly was in place, the aircraft could be towed by a small three-wheeled tractor to its dispersal. The hydraulically retractable skid helped to absorb landing shocks through a simple oleo system. As the skid retracted, the dolly, which was attached by a pair of lugs, was automatically jettisoned. There was also an emergency release if it became necessary. (EN Archive)

deliver a promised alternative engine, Messerschmitt eventually settled on the Me 163B being fitted with an improved Walter 109-509 B-1 rocket engine that featured an auxiliary combustion chamber known as the *Marschofen* that was intended to improve the aircraft's duration at cruising speeds. But still progress was dogged, and by late spring 1943 Messerschmitt was forced to revise its schedule because of delays to flight-testing and a manpower shortage stemming from demand overload on the company for both the Me 163 and the Me 262 jet interceptor.

There had also been some diversion caused by Professor Messerschmitt proposing the incorporation of a V-tail on the Me 163B, which he felt would aid lift during bank and landing maneuvers and allow for a larger center-of-gravity margin. He also recommended the fitting of part-span or possibly full-span landing flaps that could also be used to increase lift. There was some wrangling between Messerschmitt and Lippisch, the former annoyed with the latter because of his tendency to engage in direct communication with the RLM over projects without ratification from Messerschmitt officials.

At least the production situation was relieved to some extent by an agreement with Hanns Klemm Flugzeugbau GmbH at Stuttgart-Böblingen under which Klemm would dedicate factory space and personnel for final assembly at Messerschmitt, and would also undertake some final assembly at Lechfeld commencing with the Me 163B V23 (the 23rd B-series prototype). Klemm was also to install the planned Walter rocket engine.

The entire tail assembly of Me 163B V53 Wk-Nr 16310062 has been removed to expose the HWK RII 211 rocket motor (RLM designation 109-509A-1 or B) for servicing. A motor unit could be removed by releasing bolts that attached it to the fuselage frame. In August 1944, this aircraft, with the tactical code "White 9," is known to have been flown by Unteroffizier Kurt Schiebeler of 1./JG 400 from Brandis. (EN Archive)

"Yellow 13" was assigned to
7./JG 400 at Husum in April 1945.
Generally, the camouflage
schemes applied to Me 163s were
"variations on a theme,"
depending on the manufacturer,
time of build, and unit. The
scheme on this aircraft was
representative of a style used
towards the end of the war, with
heavy mottling, probably of RLM
82 *Hellgrün* over a base fuselage
color of RLM 78 *Hellblau*. On the
upper vertical stabilizer and
rudder, the pattern is more of a
"tiger stripe," while the upper
wing surfaces were RLM 81
(*Braunviolett*)/82 splinter
pattern. The nose was in the
Staffel color of yellow.

On March 1, 1943, Hauptmann Wolfgang Späte, the commander of E.Kdo 16, the dedicated test unit established by the Luftwaffe in April 1942 to test and assess the Me 163 as a combat aircraft, wrote to Generalmajor Adolf Galland, the *General der Jagdflieger*, expressing his concern that basic changes to the airframe were required as a result of the latest estimates of equipment weight and center-of-gravity position. Then, on the 26th, as Department "L" was absorbed into the Messerschmitt business, Lippisch, unhappy with such a situation, resigned and left the company 48 hours later.

E.Kdo 16 received a batch of early-production Me 163B-0 models which had, at least in part, been fitted with a pair of 20mm MG 151 cannon in the wing roots and redesignated as the Me 163B-1a, although the designation B-0/R2 is also believed to have been used. In its final, operational form, however, as built by Klemm, the single-seat Me 163B was produced as the B-1 (or B-1a), featuring a semi-monocoque fuselage of stressed-skin light alloy with an almost circular cross-section, distorted by large fairings between the wings and the fuselage aft of the canopy and for the ventral landing skid. The rear of the skid housed two lugs that had mechanical catches and which secured the two-wheel take-off dolly. The Me 163B-1a was just 5.85m in length, and on its dolly it was 2.76m at its maximum height.

The wings were swept back by 23.3 degrees on the quarter-chord line and were constructed of wood with 8mm plywood skin covered with doped fabric over main and auxiliary spars bolted to the fuselage. The span was 9.33m. Fitted to the trailing edges were fabric-covered elevons which gave lateral and longitudinal control, with large trimming flaps inboard of the elevons. The flaps were forward of these at mid-chord. The fixed slots of 2.13m in length on the leading edges as designed by Lippisch took up roughly half of the outer span of each wing and terminated about 30cm from the wingtip. The total wing area was 18.50 sq. m.

The wings also contained the *C-Stoff* tanks, each wing accommodating a leading edge tank of 73-liter capacity and a main tank of 173-liter capacity.

The pilot was accommodated in an unpressurized cockpit from which there was very good all-round visibility and which was protected by medium armor steel plate for his head, shoulders, and back. There was also an armored steel nose cone, at the tip of which was a mini propeller that drove an electrical supply generator.

Either side of the pilot's seat was a small, self-sealing fuel tank to contain 60 liters of *T-Stoff*, with another main tank for this fuel type of 1,040-liter capacity located behind the cockpit. Behind this was a bi-fuel Walter 109-509A-2 rocket motor providing around 1,700kg of thrust. The aircraft's maximum speed was 830km/h at sea level and 955km/h between 3,000–9,000m. The climbing time to 9,000m was 2.6 mins and 12,000m was reached in 3.35 mins. The normal radius of action was 35.5km at 800km/h.

The MG 151s of the Me 163B-1a, the barrels of which protruded from the wing root, were replaced by a pair of shorter-barreled 30mm Rheinmetall-Borsig MK 108 cannon as standard in the wing roots, each with 120 rounds per gun. The pilot used these weapons with a Revi 16B gunsight.

By late 1943, the Messerschmitt factory at Obertraubling was required for the output of Bf 109 fighters, so production of the Me 163 was transferred fully to Klemm at Böblingen. The first delivery of a powered Me 163B did not take place until January 1944, a delay mainly attributable to the lack of engines.

Me 163B *KOMET*

5.85m

2.76m

9.33m

THE STRATEGIC SITUATION

Apposite to the strategic situation forming the backdrop to this book is a comment by historian Richard Overy in his study of the European bombing war of 1939–45:

> When Allied bombing was finally directed at oil production in May 1944, the threat to the vulnerable capital-intensive sectors of German industry could only be solved by finding effective ways of sheltering it from the bombs, or giving up the conflict.

Indeed, the importance of synthetic oil to the German war effort in 1944 cannot be overstated, and nor can the risk posed to it by the Allied joint strategic bombing campaign that had been waged with increasing force since the early autumn of 1943. Allied commanders recognized that along with other industry, transportation, and military infrastructure, oil was a key target.

As part of the series of economic measures known as the Four Year Plan, the Nazis cultivated development and support for the German synthetic fuel industry in 1939. This was necessary because since going to war, Germany's oil supplies had diminished. The country had consumed 7.5 million tons of petroleum products, of which two-thirds had been imported. The invasion of Poland had left stocks so low that only a further six months of operations could be sustained. The situation was compensated by further conquest in the West in 1940 and the support of Axis allies, meaning that the resources of France, Hungary, and Rumania were brought into Germany's supply orbit.

However, the Nazis recognized that something more would be needed to – quite literally – fuel their war ambitions, and so a massive development program got underway to produce synthetic oil from coal using the Bergius and Fischer-Tropsch processes of hydrogenation.

These initiatives saw the lignite mines of the Sudetenland consolidated into one large company called the Sudetenländische Bergbau AG based in Brüx in the northern Sudetenland. Lignite (or brown coal) was a feedstock for synthetic fuel, and as such, in October 1939, Reichsmarschall Hermann Göring set about developing what was planned to be the largest synthetic oil plant at Brüx known as the Sudetenländische Triebstoffwerke AG, controlled by the Reichswerke industrial conglomerate which lay under Göring's supervision and which acted as a trustee for the Reich. The abundance of lignite in a location assumed to be well out of reach of any prospective attack by Allied bombers probably influenced this development.

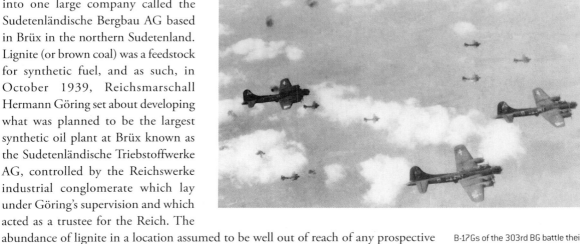

B-17Gs of the 303rd BG battle their way through "Flak-infested skies" on their way to Berlin on March 6, 1944. Despite heavy losses throughout 1943 and early 1944, the USAAF was able to draw upon America's economic and industrial strength, and its comparative wealth in manpower, to maintain its daylight bombing onslaught against the Third Reich. From the spring of 1944, a part of this air power was directed at Nazi Germany's centers of oil production and, in this regard, the 303rd BG would encounter Me 163s as the latter sought to defend them from attack. (Author's Collection)

By April 1944, however, after Germany had been fighting a war for five years, the Third Reich's crucial supply of oil from its ally, Rumania, had been cut off, severely negating the prospect of continuing any form of effective, large-scale mobile warfare. Thus Nazi Germany became ever more dependent on its synthetic fuel production and industry, which it had developed significantly since 1939.

The Fischer-Tropsch process group of nine synthetic plants, for example, supplied 500,000 tons per annum, and in 1943 total output from all the plants amounted to more than 6,180,000 tons of petroleum products. By early 1944 such was the total production of synthetic oil that it gave the German political and military authorities reason for confidence. Paradoxically, set against the loss of Rumanian oil was the fact that April 1944 saw the highest output of synthetic aviation fuel, but also the final month where production exceeded consumption.

A number of key production plants and refineries were clustered around the city of Leipzig in Saxony, 175km northeast of Brüx. These included the Bergius hydrogenation process Ammoniawerke Merseburg GmbH at Leuna (Merseburg), Wintershall AG at Lützkendorf, Braunkohle-Benzin AG at Böhlen and Zeitz, the Fischer-Tropsch process Braunkohle-Benzin AG at Ruhland, the Saechsische Werke at Mölbis, which produced Benzol, the Deutsche Petroleum AG refinery at Rositz, the Rhenania Ossag Mineraloelwerke AG refinery at Freital, and a major oil storage facility at Riesa.

On April 19, 1944, Gen Dwight D. Eisenhower authorized Brig Gen Carl Spaatz, commander of US Strategic Air Forces in Europe, to proceed with a limited bombing offensive against German oil production using the US Eighth Air Force. Encouraged, Spaatz ordered the Eighth Air Force's commander, Lt Gen James "Jimmy" Doolittle, to begin attacking as many oil targets as possible in central Germany.

Although this photograph of the bomb-damaged synthetic fuel plant at Leuna-Merseburg was taken immediately post-war on May 12, 1945, it illustrates the size and scale of development of the complex and others like it. (Alamy)

OPPOSITE

This map shows Me 163 principal operational target defense airfields and the key refinery and hydrogenation production plants the *Komet* pilots were tasked with defending.

After delays caused by resources being diverted to attacking the V-weapons' infrastructure, as well as a period of adverse weather, on May 12, 1944, 572 B-17 Flying Fortresses and 242 B-24 Liberators bombed the plants at Brüx, Böhlen, Lützkendorf, Merseburg, Zeitz, and another oil target further south at Zwickau. Although the targets were obscured by low cloud and ground haze, a total of 1,718 tons of bombs fell on the German oil plants. Brüx, Böhlen, and Zeitz were temporarily placed out of operation. Despite suffering heavy losses in bombers, the USAAF viewed the mission as a successful opening to the campaign.

The Americans returned on May 28, sending more than 400 bombers to attack the plants at Merseburg-Leuna, Lützkendorf, Ruhland, and Zeitz, the latter being rendered inoperative again. Just under a month later, on June 20, the Eighth Air Force despatched its largest raid to date – a force of 1,361 bombers, escorted by 729 fighters, struck at oil targets in northern and central Germany. Once more key plants were forced to shut down to conduct repairs.

Despite attacks against German oil production by early July 1944 being described by the official history as "a purely marginal and even somewhat haphazard affair" within the framework of the Allied bombing offensive, intent was shown on July 9 when a joint Anglo-American oil targets committee was formed to monitor the Axis

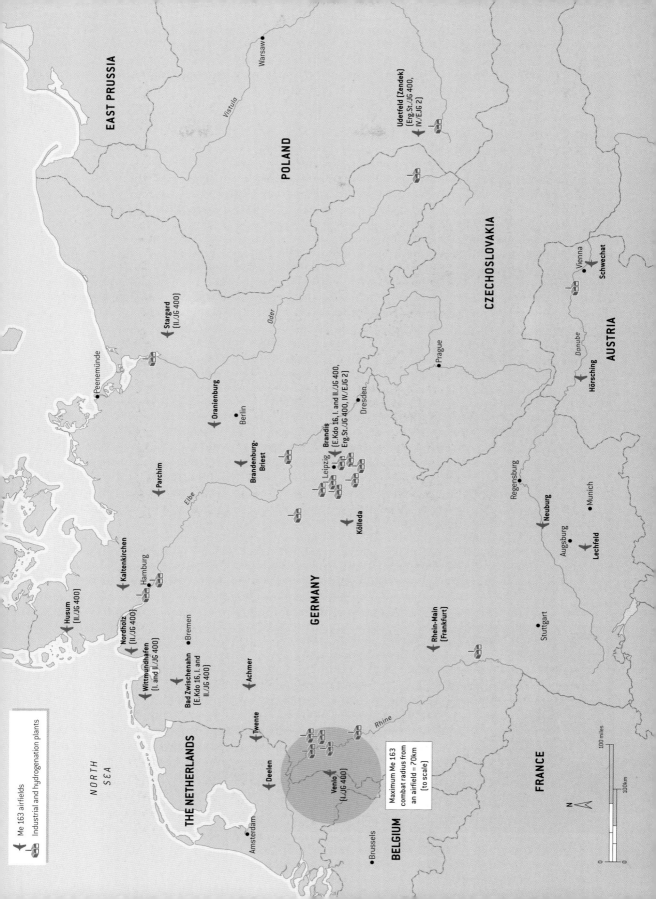

Me 163 airfields

Industrial and hydrogenation plants

NORTH SEA

THE NETHERLANDS

Amsterdam

Brussels

BELGIUM

FRANCE

EAST PRUSSIA

Vistula

Warsaw

POLAND

Oder

CZECHOSLOVAKIA

Prague

AUSTRIA

Danube

Vienna

Schwechat

Hörsching

Peenemünde

Stargard
[II./JG 400]

Oranienburg

Berlin

Parchim

Brandenburg-
Briest

Brandis
[E.Kdo 16, I. and II./JG 400,
Erg.St./JG 400, IV./EJG 2]

Leipzig

Dresden

Kölleda

Regensburg

Neuburg

Augsburg

Munich

Lechfeld

Stuttgart

Husum
[II./JG 400]

Nordholz
[II./JG 400]

Wittmundhafen
[I. and II./JG 400]

Kaltenkirchen

Hamburg

Bremen

Bad Zwischenahn
[E.Kdo 16, I. and
II./JG 400]

Achmer

Elbe

GERMANY

Rhein-Main
[Frankfurt]

Rhine

Twente

Deelen

Venlo
[I./JG 400]

Udetfeld [Zendek]
[Erg.St./JG 400,
IV./EJG 2]

Maximum Me 163
combat radius from
an airfield = 70km
(to scale)

100 miles

100km

N

oil situation, to assess damage inflicted by bombing and to determine future target strategy and priorities.

That month in Germany, Hitler had promised his Reichsminister for Armaments and War Production, Albert Speer, that there would be more fighters to provide cover for the hydrogenation plants. According to Speer, already 150,000 workers had been assigned to rebuilding the damage inflicted by the USAAF's daylight- and the RAF's night-bombers. Many of these workers were skilled, and their value was better served producing tanks. Yet there was the dichotomy, for as Speer wrote, "it would be pointless to have tanks if we could not produce enough fuel."

To defend the plants around Leipzig, the Luftwaffe marshaled its fighter forces under the command of I. *Jagdkorps*, led by Generalleutnant Josef Schmid, headquartered at Braunschweig-Querem (Treuenbrietzen from April 1, 1944). The *Korps*, in turn, comprised five *Jagddivision* – 1., 2., 3., 7., and 8. – along with two local sector commands, the *Jagdabschnittsführer Mittelrhein* and the *Jagdfliegerführer Ostmark*, these latter commands being headquarters of brigade status and controlling day and nightfighter units within a sub-area of a *Jagddivision*.

The *Jagdkorps* commanded all day and nightfighter units employed in the *Reichsverteidigung* (Air Defense of the Reich), as well as the signals units attached to the radar ground organization and the radio intercept and aircraft reporting service. Each *Jagddivision* coordinated the operations of day and nightfighter units within a given geographical sector, as well as the posting of air situation maps on the basis of reports submitted by the radio intercept service and branches of the aircraft warning service.

The *Jagddivision* responsible for the Leipzig area – and thus the protection of the synthetic oil plants – was 1. *Jagddivision* based at Döberitz, since late March 1944 under the command of Oberst Hajo Herrmann. This command covered northwest and central Germany and the area east of the Elbe River – effectively the central approach over the Reich for bombers coming from the west.

On May 12, I. *Jagdkorps* was able to send up 465 single-engined fighters from 22 *Jagdgruppen*, along with 40 twin-engined *Zerstörer*, representing the greatest defensive effort by the Luftwaffe of the war to date. Although the USAAF lost 55 bombers and ten fighters, as mentioned earlier, the Eighth Air Force viewed it as a positive mission. When the Americans made their second raid against the oil plants on the 28th, they clashed with 250 fighters from I. *Jagdkorps*, of which a major element came from 1. *Jagddivision*. The Eighth Air Force lost 33 bombers, including 15 from one combat wing near Magdeburg which was flying without escort. More than 300 bomber aircrew were lost, as well as 17 fighters. The Luftwaffe had 50 aircraft shot down and 23 pilots killed, with a further 14 wounded.

In the next big assault, on June 20, B-17s from the 3rd Bombardment Division (BD) bombed the Braunkohle-Benzin AG plant at Magdeburg-Rothensee. The diary of I. *Jagdkorps* noted that the attack on the "Brabag" plant took place in conditions of good visibility, in eight waves, over just seven minutes shortly after 0900 hrs. The *Korps* put up 167 single- and twin-engined fighters from 1., 7., and 8. *Jagddivision* in two main attacks, of which 115 engaged in combat. Twin-engined Me 410 *Zerstörer* of II./ZG 76 were directed by 8. *Jagddivision* to attack the 3rd BD over Magdeburg.

But the B-17s were defended by a strong escort screen, and only three bombers and two P-51s were claimed downed. In total, the USAAF lost 54 bombers and 15 fighters that day, although in terms of the bombers, this represented just four percent of those that were active over occupied territory. In the area of I. *Jagdkorps*, 34 aircraft were lost, with 26 pilots killed or reported as missing in action and another 19 wounded. After the raid, I. *Jagdkorps* reported that:

> Considerable damage was caused to all the factories of the oil industry which were hit by the bombing. This applies particularly to the hydrogenation plant at Pölitz, the "Brabag" factories at Magdeburg and to the Rhenania Ossag factories at Hamburg.

Attrition from the oil raids was draining both sides in this mighty aerial contest. By mid-July, however, the Luftwaffe was able to introduce a new, promising element in its battle to defend the skies over the vital Leipzig-area oil plants, specifically those at Leuna. Commencing around July 10, a new fighter *Staffel*, 1./JG 400, initially under the command of Oberleutnant Rudolf Opitz, but recently taken over by Hauptmann Robert Olejnik, began relocating from Wittmundhafen to Brandis, an airfield on low-lying land just a few kilometers east of Leipzig, and therefore ideally located for covering the defense of the plants. Not only that, the aircraft which equipped the *Staffel* was the new Me 163 rocket-powered point interceptor.

Although few in number, the tactical advantage of the *Komet* (the name by which the Me 163 had become known) was its ability to be scrambled quickly and to climb fast and high from airfields close to the bombers' target, and to attack a bomber formation at speed with impunity. The transfer from Wittmundhafen must have made quite a spectacle, as the futuristic-looking interceptors were air-towed by Bf 110 tugs to Brandis. As a precaution, each Bf 110 carried a spare undercarriage dolly for its Me 163 in case they were forced to make a landing en route. At least 11 rocket fighters are believed to have been transported this way from Wittmundhafen.

There would be little time for "settling in," however. The Me 163's baptism of fire was just days away.

Oberfeldwebel Friedrich Ferdinand Reukauf of I./JG 400 snatches a few moments of rest in the sunshine on the wing of an Me 163B parked at readiness. Reukauf was a former glider pilot and instructor who taught future Me 163 pilots on the *Stummelhabicht* glider and in air gunnery, but he would lose his life flying the Me 163 when shot down by a Mustang from the 359th FG on March 15, 1945. The aircraft seen here carries the emblem of 1. *Staffel*, and its nose is adorned in the unit color of white. Note the starting cart that is plugged in and the pilot's flight helmet and oxygen tube lying over the canopy support frame. The canopy was made of 90mm-thick armored glass. (Ransom Collection)

THE COMBATANTS

Me 163 PILOT TRAINING

To prepare the first pilots for operations on the Me 163, in April 1942 orders were issued to form a dedicated testing and evaluation unit to be known as E.Kdo 16. It was initially established at Göttingen and placed under the command of the experienced fighter ace and Knight's Cross-holder Hauptmann Wolfgang Späte. The *Kommando* moved variously to Augsburg, Peenemünde-West, and Kiel in May, with Späte, clad in a white protective suit, making his first take-off in an Me 163A on the 11th following some brief words of instruction by Heini Dittmar, who told him to "Just fly off." Dittmar also indicated to Späte where he should park his aircraft after landing – at a spot where the grass had been burnt away by *Z-Stoff*.

Over the coming weeks, Späte and his small staff scoured the Luftwaffe's fighter arm for men who were known to be proficient former glider pilots, and they also called in at least two civilian pilots with similar experience. By the summer, the initial cadre included some well-known names with considerable and varied operational experience, such as the Knight's Cross-holder Oberleutnant Joschi Pöhs, an Austrian veteran who had flown with Späte in JG 54. He had been with that *Geschwader* since the Polish campaign (when the *Gruppe* was I./JG 76), then seen service over France, England, and in the Balkans. Pöhs received the Knight's Cross on August 6, 1941 while with 5./JG 54, having claimed 28 victories in 225 operational missions.

There was also Oberleutnant Johannes Kiel, a *Zerstörer* pilot who had been awarded the Knight's Cross on March 18, 1942 in recognition of his 20 victories. Like Pöhs, he had flown over Poland, where he served with 3./JGr 102. Kiel was shot down over France on April 7, 1940, bailed out and was captured. Released at the conclusion of

the French campaign, he was posted to 3.*Staffel* of *Zestörergeschwader* (ZG) 26 and took part in operations over England flying Bf 110s. He was appointed *Staffelkapitän* of his *Staffel* in April 1941, before flying in the campaigns in the Balkans, over Crete, and in Russia. Kiel was credited with the destruction of nine tanks, 20 guns, 16 railway engines, three transport convoys, and 62 aircraft on the ground, as well as the sinking of one submarine, three fast patrol boats, and one transport ship, all near the island of Ösel (Saaremaa), off the coast of Estonia. He became *Staffelkapitän* of 6./ZG 2 in May 1942 and joined E.Kdo 16 in October of that same year.

Also assigned to E.Kdo 16 were Hauptmann Anton "Toni" Thaler and Oberleutnant Herbert Langer. Thaler was a Stuka pilot who had been posted to *Stukageschwader* (StG) 51 in August 1939. Promoted to oberleutnant on October 1, 1940, he was with 4./StG 1 by July 1941. Thaler remained with the *Staffel* until May 1942, when he joined StG 3, followed by I./StG 5 three months later. After a lengthy period of combat operations, he was posted to a seaplane repair factory at Bari, in Italy, in November 1942, where he remained until January 1943. After a brief spell as a test pilot at the Focke-Wulf plant at Marienburg, Thaler joined E.Kdo 16 at Peenemünde as a flying instructor on April 15, 1943.

Oberleutnant Herbert Langer joined E.Kdo 16 from a *Frontflieger-Sammelgruppe* (operational pilots depot) at the end of April 1943. After a period of glider training, his abilities were sufficient enough to prompt Späte to appoint him as a flying instructor alongside Thaler.

During this time, aircraft trickled into E.Kdo16, including, eventually, ten powered Me 163As. On June 13, a group of senior officials arrived at Peenemünde comprised of Generalfeldmarschall Erhard Milch (the Secretary of State for Air and the Generalluftzeugmeister), Albert Speer and Generalmajor Adolf Galland. They were visiting to watch the first formation take-off by three Me 163As, led by Späte

Groundcrew work on two Me 163As delivered to E.Kdo 16 outside the hangars at Peenemünde in the summer of 1943. At left is what appears to be V8 CD+IM and at right is V6 CD+IK. The ability to undertake such work would be rudely disrupted by the British bombing of Peenemünde in August of that year. (Ransom Collection)

Leutnant (later Hauptmann) Rudolf "Rudi" Opitz, clad in a protective flying suit, talks with Leutnant Josef Pöhs, while behind can be seen Me 163A V10 Wk-Nr 1630000007 CD+IO during flight tests at Peenemünde in July 1943. Opitz's flying suit, as well as his boots and gloves, were made of a non-organic material to avoid the risk of fire to which organic clothing would have been susceptible. Opitz served with E.Kdo 16 before being appointed, successively, Kommandeur of I. and II./JG 400. (Ransom Collection)

accompanied by Opitz and Pöhs. It was a successful demonstration. The rocket fighters streaked upwards into the sky, climbing quickly and disappearing from view. It seems Milch, Speer, and Galland departed with favorable impressions.

In late 1942, the *Kommando* took delivery of its first non-powered Me 163B, by which stage E.Kdo 16 had become a more structured unit, with Späte as *Kommandoführer*, Pöhs as Adjutant, Thaler as Senior Technical Officer, assisted by Hauptmann Otto Böhner, and Opitz as Chief Flight Officer. The goal was to bring 30 pilots to readiness who would form a nucleus for the further development of organized, operational Me 163-equipped *Staffeln* and *Gruppen*. To this end, Oberleutnant Franz Medicus, Leutnante Hans Bott, Fritz Kelb, Franz Rösle, and Mano Ziegler, and Feldwebel Rolf Glogner joined the *Kommando*, as did Oberleutnant Otto Oertzen, an engineer from the Walter Werke, who would oversee engine matters.

At this time, initial training for preparation for the Me 163A took place at a glider pilots' school, where pupils commenced instruction, often closely observed by Opitz, on a dual-control DFS *Kranich* (Crane) glider. They then moved on to the Grunau Baby and the Rhönsperber, followed by the shorter wingspan DFS *Stummel Habicht* (Stubby Hawk) glider, which had more aerobatic qualities and a landing speed of 100km/h, mirroring that of the Me 163A.

On the night of August 17–18, 1943, RAF Bomber Command launched a major raid on Peenemünde. Although heavy damage affected mainly the residential areas of the test complex, to continue its training, E.Kdo 16 was forced to relocate 500 km west to Bad Zwischenahn, where the bulk of conversion training was carried out, and where the unit hoped to receive the first powered Me 163B production machine.

In his monthly report for December 1943, Späte noted:

In the period covered by this report, only 12 days could be used for training because of prevailing bad weather, and even then not the whole of the day. Despite this situation, 280 towed starts and 68 powered take-offs were made.

It was noticed recently that the pilots' performance was better the more practice they had had with gliders. A few gliding flights are enough in almost all cases to maintain his prowess during interruptions in training on the Me 163 resulting from bad weather, illness, etc. The use of *Habichts* with a reduced wing area (8m wingspan) is particularly important and valuable. These aircraft will be essential for maintaining pilots' skills at operational bases. Towed starts with the *Habicht* [glider] require much less fuel and fulfil almost the same purpose as a training flight with the Me 163, which uses 2,000kg of C- and T-Stoff. The saving in fuel alone would justify the series production of reduced-span *Habicht*.

When they were ready to fly the Me 163, trainees first went up in an A-model under tow, progressing to gliding flights with low wing loading. These would culminate in flights where the aircraft carried water ballast. Finally, a "live" or "sharp" take-off would be made in an Me 163A, which involved flying the fueled aircraft from a standing start. Once this had been mastered, the trainee pilot would graduate to the Me 163B.

This involved an

A camouflaged *Stummel Habicht* glider used for training future Me 163 pilots. The glider, with its eight-meter wingspan, was used for training after the *Kranich*. The shorter wingspan replicated the handling characteristics of the Me 163. (Ransom Collection)

extreme increase in demand on a pilot's mental and physical stamina. In the climb, flying at 800km/h and covering 4,875m per minute, the B-model could reach 9,150m in 2.6 minutes and a normal service ceiling of 12,040m in 3.35 minutes. The aircraft could fly at a maximum speed of 965km/h at between 3,050–9,150m for 3.75 minutes at full power. The landing speed of an Me 163B was considerably faster than that of the A-model, depending on how much fuel remained in the tanks following a flight.

Hauptmann Robert Olejnik, who was appointed to command 1./JG 400, recalled:

Once their conversion training on the Me 163A had been completed, the pilots were made familiar with the operational aircraft, the Me 163B. This did not take as long as the conversion training, as the Me 163B was flown in exactly the same way as the Me 163A, except that it was heavier and, because of this, had a higher landing speed. First, three towed flights with the Me 163B with empty fuel tanks were made, and then came one or two flights with the aircraft with ballast, towed by an Me 110. The Me 163B's tanks were filled with 300–400 liters of water, to simulate the weight of tanks half-filled with fuel, in order to achieve a higher speed on landing. The aircraft then had an approach speed of 250km/h and a touch-down speed of about 210–230km/h. This was about the same as that of an armed Me 163B with perhaps a small amount of fuel remaining in its tanks.

As with the Me 163A, the fuel tanks of the Me 163B were only half-filled so that they would be empty by the time the aircraft had climbed to an altitude of 4,500–5,000m. For take-off, the Me 163B was trimmed to make it tail-heavy. The thrust of the rocket engine caused the aircraft to accelerate very quickly. After take-off, the undercarriage dolly was jettisoned at a height of about 15m and then the pilot had to act at breakneck speed to retrim the aircraft for normal flight. The skid was retracted, and by the time the aircraft had reached the airfield's perimeter it was flying at 650–700km/h. The acceleration on take-off was 4.5g. The Me 163B reached a speed of over 700 km/h shortly after take-off, climbed at an angle of 60 degrees and continued accelerating.

It was always flown until the tanks were empty in order to be rid of the dangerous fuel. Once the engine had cut out, the pilot went into a routine of practicing turns and of landing on an imaginary runway, such as a wisp of cloud. The landing with an Me 163B was the same as with an Me 163A, except that speed on touch-down was slightly higher (about 210–250km/h) with the former aircraft.

Fueling the Me 163 was a vital part of the training program – aircraft cannot fly without fuel and, equally, groundcrew had to be trained sufficiently in handling the volatile fuel mix used for the rocket interceptor. Should *C-Stoff* and *T-Stoff* come into contact with one another during the fueling process, spontaneous ignition would follow. Any organic item such as normal clothing, wood, or human flesh would burn if the propellant was spilled onto it. But as late as October, there were challenges in respect to refueling, as Späte registered in E.Kdo 16's monthly report:

> The refueling of the Me 163 from open canisters can be done only under exceptional and almost unacceptable circumstances. Normally, refueling must be done with special tankers. Their development in comparison with that of the aircraft is taking far too long. *Erprobungskommando* 16 still does not have a tanker equipped with useable fuel gauges and refueling equipment. Training due to begin within the next few days will therefore face almost insurmountable difficulties.

Eventually, special three-ton Opel *Blitz* bowsers (*Stofftankwagen*) were introduced, clearly marked on their tank sides and on the rear doors covering the pump control panel with the large letters "C" or "T" applied on a white disc in a circle. The bowsers were capable of carrying up to 2,500 liters of fuel.

The standard method of fueling involved filling the Me 163 with *C-Stoff* first. The tanks for the *C-Stoff* were located in the fuselage behind the ammunition bay and in the wings. The fuel was pumped via a hose connected to the rear control panel of the bowser. A technician wearing protective rubber overalls and gloves would position himself on the wing and rest against the fuselage to unscrew the *C-Stoff* filler cap, which was on top of the rear fuselage not far from the tail assembly. A large funnel, in which was built a filter, was then placed into the filler point. Holding the nozzle at the other end of the hose over the funnel, the technician would carefully open the nozzle valve and allow the fuel to pour into the tanks. After the fueling process, all equipment used was thoroughly washed with running water to remove any propellant residue.

Me 163B *KOMET*

1. *T-Stoff* tank
2. Automatic fuel overflow pipe
3. Trim handwheel
4. Manual pump for flaps
5. Throttle lever
6. Take-off dolly emergency release handle
7. Fuel jettison handle
8. Air pressure gauge
9. Canopy latch
10. Tow-tug release handle
11. Skid and tail undercarriage lever
12. Canopy emergency release handle
13. Dolly emergency release pressure gauge
14. Main power switch
15. Armored glass windscreen
16. Revi 16B gunsight
17. Variometer (rate of climb indicator)
18. Artificial horizon
19. Airspeed indicator
20. Altimeter
21. Engine RPM counter
22. Engine temperature gauge
23. Engine thrust gauge
24. Oil pressure gauge
25. Fuel consumption gauge
26. Oxygen pressure gauge
27. Oxygen indicator gauge
28. Oxygen regulator
29. FuG 25a Erstling transponder frequency switch
30. Oxygen supply
31. Starboard equipment console
32. *T-Stoff* tank
33. Pilot's seat
34. KG 12E control column
35. Rudder pedals
36. FuG 25a Erstling transponder control unit
37. Emergency canopy release mechanism
38. Ammunition counter
39. Low fuel content warning light

A technician leans against the fuselage of an Me 163B of JG 400 in order to carefully direct pumped *C-Stoff* through a filtered funnel into the tank. The man wears a protective rubber smock and gloves. Note the fuselage access panel has been removed so as to allow access to the tank for replenishment. A second groundcrewman is watching the levels on the gauges at the rear of the bowser. (EN Archive)

T-Stoff was pumped in a similar manner into tanks located behind and alongside the pilot's cockpit, although in the case of *T-Stoff* a special nozzle and control/filler valve was used and the filler cap and point, which were located in the center section of the top fuselage, were larger. As with *C-Stoff*, after fueling with *T-Stoff* all associated equipment was washed down thoroughly.

In order to conduct an engine test, the aircraft's propellant tanks were filled with water, which was then forced under pressure through the propulsion system in order to flush out residual traces of fuel prior to removal or maintenance of the rocket motor, or should the aircraft have been stationary for extended periods between flights.

The first three production Me 163Bs arrived at Bad Zwischenahn in January 1944. Eventually, these were used to devise suitable attack tactics, but initially only towed starts were undertaken with empty or water-ballasted aircraft, and it was only Opitz who had experience in making a powered flight in the Me 163B.

Things proceeded slowly, and the sense of frustration can be detected in a surviving report of Späte's from January 1944:

The training of pilots with the already small number of Me 163As is being hampered by the unserviceability of the aircraft owing to problems with the engines and the airframe or the non-availability of spare parts. The delivery of engine components by Focke-Achgelis, Laupheim, is taking too long. The five powered take-offs with the Me 163B were made by Major Späte and Oberleutnant Opitz on January 24. These were test and acceptance flights, the take-offs being made with only half the fuel load. There were no problems with the engines. The propellant remaining after the flights was between 50–100kg of *T-Stoff* and the corresponding amount of *C-Stoff*. Finding the correct throttle lever position for setting the engine to idle is still difficult.

Trainee pilots would climb a short ladder leant against the left side of the cockpit, then slip down into the cockpit while a groundcrewman would push a parachute and safety harness over the pilot's flying suit. Parachutes were a cause for concern, as Späte explained in January 1944:

PVC-coated parachute – the first three PVC-coated parachutes have been delivered for service. This number is nowhere near enough for flight-testing of the aircraft. This type of parachute is just as essential as the pilot's protective clothing because he sits between the T-Stoff tanks, which jut out inside the cockpit. Leaking T-Stoff sets fire to a normal parachute, and this situation will render bailing out an illusion. It is requested that PVC

WOLFGANG SPÄTE

Wolfgang Späte was born on September 8, 1911 in Dresden. Like so many German youth of this period, he took up gliding, and at the age of just 16 he obtained his gliding licenses after flying regularly on the Wasserkuppe. Späte later took part in national and international gliding competitions, and in 1938 claimed victory in the Rhön competition. Having become only the seventh holder of the Performance Badge for Gliding in Gold, Späte joined the DFS in Darmstadt as a test pilot in 1937 while also studying engineering at the technical college in the city.

He commenced his wartime service with the Luftwaffe flying Hs 126 reconnaissance aircraft over Poland in September 1939 with 2.(H)/23 and then saw action in France in 1940. In early January 1941 Späte transferred to the fighter arm, joining Bf 109-equipped 5./JG 54, with whom he flew in the Balkans and on the Eastern Front. He proved a potent combat pilot and a budding unit leader, and on August 9, 1941, he was awarded the Honor Goblet by Göring. The following month Späte was appointed *Staffelkapitän* of 5./JG 54, and he was then awarded the Knight's Cross on October 5, 1941 after having claimed 45 victories. The Oak Leaves, presented personally by Hitler, followed on April 23, 1942 in recognition of his personal score reaching 72 victories. In May, Späte was assigned by the RLM as Typenbegleiter (Aircraft Type Development Coordinator) for the Me 163, although he was also sent by Generalmajor Adolf Galland to assess the Me 262 – Späte

flew the second prototype of the jet interceptor, about which he became enthusiastic.

Simultaneous to performing his role of Typenbegleiter, he was appointed commander of E.Kdo 16, a specialist testing unit formed to evaluate the Me 163 as an operational aircraft. Commencing in May 1944, for a little more than four months Späte commanded IV./JG 54 and again saw action in the West and the East flying Bf 109s and Fw 190s. In late August 1944 he became *Gruppenkommandeur* of the newly formed I./JG 400 at Brandis, the first *Gruppe* to fly the *Komet* operationally. With formation of a II.*Gruppe*, the then Major Späte became *Kommodore* of JG 400 from late November 1944.

In April 1945, lacking the specialized rocket fuel, suitably trained pilots, and transport, JG 400 was wound down, with the *Geschwaderstab* being dissolved. Späte was transferred to take command of I./JG 7 equipped with the Me 262. He later recalled, "I thought it would offer me the best opportunity to engage myself in the final defense of our country." He ended the war credited with 99 victories.

Post-war, Späte worked as a test pilot for the *Armée de l'Air* and, later, as director of a photographic company. Between 1956–67, he served with the reformed Luftwaffe, holding the rank of oberstleutnant. From 1967 to 1971, Späte worked with Alexander Lippisch flight-testing his surface-skimming aircraft. In retirement he became an aviation journalist. He died at Edewicht on April 30, 1997.

Oberleutnant Wolfgang Späte, at right, with two other Knight's Cross-holders who would become involved with the Me 163 – at left is Oberleutnant Johannes Kiel and, center, Leutnant Josef Pöhs. The three pilots were photographed in June 1942, having "gone back to school" to receive glider training in preparation for flying the rocket interceptor. (Ransom Collection)

OPPOSITE

A posed but nevertheless excellent color photograph of SSgt Frank T. Lusic, from Illinois, a B-17 gunner clad in typical sheepskin-lined flight gear and swathed in a "bandolier" of 0.50-cal. machine gun ammunition. He also wears a lifejacket, parachute harness, and a silk scarf. The plugs for his electrically heated suit are visible protruding from the sleeves of his flight jacket. Behind Lusic is B-17F 42-29524 "MEAT" HOUND of the 423rd BS/306th BG, at Thurleigh, in Bedfordshire, in 1943. The bomber was later transferred to the 303rd BG and was badly shot up by an enemy aircraft over Oschersleben on January 11, 1944. Although his crew bailed out, pilot 1Lt Jack W. Watson managed to fly the badly damaged and burning B-17 back to England. (Author's Collection)

parachutes are delivered to E.Kdo 16 as quickly as possible, and delivery schedules be modified bearing in mind the needs of operational units. The production of only 50 such parachutes, as E.Kdo 16 has learnt, is totally inadequate for future needs.

Once in the cockpit, the pilot would plug in his radio connections, switch on the electrics, and then pull his goggles over his eyes. Controls, flaps, and elevator trim were tested, and oxygen supply to the pilot's mask checked. The groundcrewman then lowered the canopy and the pilot would lock it from the inside.

With the throttle at idle, the pilot depressed the starter button that activated the *T-Stoff* steam turbine. The gravity-feed catalytic starter replaced the electrically-driven starter fitted to earlier rocket motors. The catalytic starter generated steam by allowing *T-Stoff* to flow over stones contained in a tank located above the engine. The *T-Stoff* was tapped from the main fuel line and entered the tank via a valve which was connected to the throttle lever in the cockpit. The steam generated by the catalytic process was fed to the turbine, which pumped fuel to the engine's combustion chamber. Because the process was purely chemical, there was no need for the battery that was used for the electrically-driven starter. The ram air-driven generator installed in the nose of the aircraft, therefore, became the only source of power for all of the aircraft's systems.

After a few seconds, with the motor firing, the pilot released the starter button and moved the throttle to First Stage, then to Second Stage, checking his instruments, then to Third Stage or full thrust. The aircraft jumped forward over its chocks and commenced its take-off run.

Once off the ground, the dolly was jettisoned at between six and ten meters. At around 650km/h, the aircraft commenced its steep climb. Pilots had to be careful to avoid leveling out while the motor was at maximum thrust because doing so was dangerous due to compressibility. The lack of air resistance at high altitude meant that at 12,000m, an Me 163B could accelerate from 400km/h to around 965km/h in just a few seconds.

Perhaps not surprisingly, the unit did suffer casualties during its training period. On November 30, 1943, Oberfeldwebel Alois Wörndl crashed at Bad Zwischenahn in Me 163A V6 CD+IK. Späte believed the loss to be as a result of "disregard for flying regulations." On December 30 Oberleutnant Pöhs was killed shortly after take-off in Me 163A V8 CD+IM. The aircraft's engine had cut out, and it was not high enough for Pöhs to bail out safely. He banked the aircraft in a steep turn back toward the airfield, but clipped the control tower. The wing of the *Komet* dug into the ground, the aircraft cartwheeled, and then exploded. It was later discovered that the undercarriage dolly had bounced higher than usual after being jettisoned, struck the underside of the aircraft and split a *T-Stoff* line. Pöhs was credited with 43 victories, of which 40 had been claimed on the Eastern Front.

Training was affected by adverse weather in February 1944, and the periods of good weather that there were saw an increased level of activity on the part of enemy aircraft. Eighty-six flights were made in the Me 163A and 82 in the Me 163B.

In early March 1944, the first Me 163Bs were used to form 1./JG 400 under the command of Hauptmann Robert Olejnik, which transferred to Wittmundhafen on the 1st of the month. Olejnik had flown an Me 163B for the first time in February.

USAAF AIR GUNNERY TRAINING

For a gunner aboard a USAAF bomber of the Eighth Air Force to attempt to fire at and hit such a *fast-moving* enemy aircraft as the Me 163 required considerable awareness, skill, and a quick understanding of range, speed, trajectory, and deflection. Sometimes, for those luckier gunners, these attributes were innate, but for most they were nurtured through a careful process of training.

Before the appearance of P-47 Thunderbolts with drop tanks from the fall of 1943, and later P-51s, which could escort bombers to deep penetration targets in Germany, the defense of a B-17 Flying Fortress was its guns, and their correct use was vital to the survival of its crew when under fighter attack. This was illustrated in stark terms by the Las Vegas Army Air Field (LVAAF) Year Book of the same year, which recorded the role of the air gunner:

> The protection they provide is vital to the success of long-range bombing. On this ability of self-protection, long-range bombing is built. Each bomber, alone, must be able to hold its own against fighters. Everything depends on the ability of one special class of men, the aerial gunners. They have to be good or they are dead, and heavy bombardment is dead with them. The five men who handle the guns in a bomber crew of nine are trained as mechanics, radio operators, cameramen. Many of them have never fired a gun. In order to make them first-rate gunners, the Air Forces give them the toughest six weeks of training in the Army.
>
> At the special schools, they learn their deadly business. Taught precision on miniature ranges with 0.22-cal. rifles, they learn to lead and swing while shooting trap and skeet. They fire machine guns, find out the trick of the turrets, have special training on altitude flying and, when their course is finished, they are assigned to operational training units ready for combat.
>
> If straws point to the wind, Las Vegas Air Field is one straw in the Nation's military program and progress that bespeaks a storm of trouble and discomfort for the enemy.

This self-belief was neither ill-founded nor exaggerated. At the beginning of the war in Europe, the USAAC had no training facilities for aerial gunnery, but in the summer of 1941, a group of officers was sent to Britain to seek guidance on how to set up such a school. Subsequently, future B-17 air gunners would arrive at the Flexible Gunnery School north of Las Vegas, in Nevada, which provided training in moveable, as opposed to fixed, guns of the type to be found on a heavy bomber. The first thing that struck most trainees arriving at the airfield was the searing heat and the inhospitable Nevada landscape. As one man recalled, "All you can see is desert sand and mountains, mile upon mile."

Here, future gunners would practice using rifles for marksmanship, shooting at clay pigeons on the ground and from moving trucks, before firing machine guns on the

Newly arrived in England, freshly trained B-17 aircrew are instructed in the art of formation flying by a senior officer using wooden models. Disciplined flying and maintaining formation was key to survival in the skies over occupied Europe. (Author's Collection)

ground. The student then graduated to the ground turret, with machine guns mounted in a turret from which they fired at towed flags. Finally, they would fire in the air from B-34 Lexingtons and B-26 Marauders. Most of the course was dedicated to the 0.50-cal. Browning M2 machine gun, the weapon they would use in the skies over Europe. Trainees were taught how to strip a gun down, and then – under test conditions – to reassemble the 80 or so parts blindfolded.

When about two-thirds of the way through the course, trainees were transferred to another facility in the same state at Indian Springs, where there would be a brief period of airborne gunnery training on AT-6 Texans using ammunition filled with different colored paint to assess individual accuracy and scoring. Finally, they would return to Las Vegas and be introduced to the B-17.

On average, during the second half of World War II, 600 gunnery students graduated from the LVAAF every five weeks, although during 1943 the school graduated 9,117 gunners. By September 1944, 227,827 gunners had been trained.

So it was that upon transfer to the European Theater of Operations, gunners *seemed* highly skilled and knew their aircraft inside and out. Initially, however, it had not been easy in England. The truth was that general standards of nose and waist position air gunnery were poor – despite high claims made during the initial clashes with the Luftwaffe. Incidents of damage from friendly fire were also not uncommon. The effective use of a heavy, reverberating 0.50-cal. gun in a 200mph slipstream against a small, fast-moving target presented enormous challenges.

Following the arrival of the first bomb groups from the US in 1942, Brig Gen Eaker and VIII Bomber Command set up further intensive gunnery training courses on land and coastal ranges procured from the British such as those near Snettisham, in Norfolk, and in Cornwall, and by acquiring a handful of target-towing aircraft, but the standards of air gunnery remained disappointing for the rest of the year. Even as late as November 1944, the Eighth Air Force conceded that:

There appears to be a serious weakness in nose gunnery. This is seen in the steady growth of the percentage of nose attacks, since enemy fighters may be expected to attack weak spots. There are explanations for this weakness: (1) the navigators and bombardiers have other primary duties, and tend to neglect their duty as gunners; (2) a high percentage of the navigators and bombardiers have had no gunnery training whatsoever.

However, by the time new B-17 groups arrived in numbers in England for the Eighth Air Force during the winter of 1943–44, operational training had reached considerably higher standards, much of it being handled by Combat Crew Replacement Centers. Ad hoc forms of training continued to be meted out at unit-level, however – for example, in April 1944, inventive gunnery officers at Kimbolton, in Cambridgeshire, constructed their own timber rig in a blister hangar into which were fitted chin, ball, and top turrets and nose gun positions from wrecked B-17s. Target images were then projected onto a screen for gunners to aim at. Elsewhere on the airfield, a B-17 top turret was fitted to the back of a truck, which would then be driven along a perimeter track so that the new gunner could practice his aim against friendly aircraft flying over the airfield.

At the time B-17s began to encounter Me 163s in the sky over central Germany from May 1944, the standard defensive gun in the Flying Fortress was the air-cooled 0.50-cal. Browning M2 machine gun. On a B-17G, the armament comprised three single 0.50-cal. flexible gun installations, three power-driven turrets with twin guns, and one manually operated, indirectly sighted twin gun installation. The Browning M2 fired 580–750 shots per minute, or around 14 shots per second. The muzzle velocity was 1,977mph/2,900ft per second. As the *Gunner's Information File* published by the Training HQ of the USAAF in May 1944 so graphically described:

> In tests on the proving ground, the caliber 0.50 smashes through the metal skin and framework of an airplane, drills through a metal ammunition box, penetrates a hard pine board – and still has enough power left to pierce a plate of armor nearly a half-inch thick.

By virtue of its method of operation, an Me 163 would dive down through an enemy bomber formation. Therefore, the most advantageous position for defense against it was the upper/top turret. The B-17G was fitted with a powered Sperry A-1 or A-1-A upper, or top turret, the latter version featuring some minor improvements over the former, but in essential form, they were the same turret. It was located in the upper section of the fuselage, just behind the pilot's compartment, and its role was to defend the whole top area of the aircraft.

The turret was installed with, as mentioned, two 0.50-cal. Browning M2 machine guns, and was operated hydraulically on pressure built up by a constant speed electric motor. It was able to turn 360 degrees in azimuth (6,400 mils). In elevation, the guns could be lowered and raised from a little below the horizontal (-5 degrees) to almost straight upwards (85 degrees – 1,509 mils). This was distinctly advantageous when defending against an enemy fighter, such as an Me 163, making a downward, diving attack. The electric motor operated both systems.

The best way for gunners to learn about their guns was to strip their weapons down and clean and maintain them themselves. It was a familiar and repeated drill. Here, gunners clean the various parts of their 0.50-cal. Browning M2 machine guns. Note the barrels have been marked up for their respective mounts in the radio, right chin, left chin, and left nose positions. (Author's Collection)

Reality – B-17s head out towards enemy territory. The Flying Fortresses would fly in self-defending formations comprised of six-aircraft squadrons, within combat boxes and wings. This view would be similar to that seen by the pilot of an Me 163B as he approached a *"Pulk"* of bombers from above and behind, his speed being his defense against an array of waist, top, tail, and ball turret machine guns. (Author's Collection)

The guns were mounted to be fed from within the turret, the right gun from the left and the left weapon from the right. They were held in their cradles by rear trunnion blocks and slides and two front trunnion studs. Ejection chutes were installed on the outside of the guns to carry away links. For protection, an oblong plate panel on the aircraft's bulkhead just aft of the turret covered the most vital part of the gunner's body in combat.

To enter the turret, the gunner – who was also the flight engineer, responsible for the in-flight monitoring and performance of the engines and other mechanical and technical systems, as well as fuel, guns, and bomb racks – would do so from the pilot's compartment by simply stepping up onto the turret's circular platform. On a bombing mission, however, he would have to approach the turret from the opposite side, over the bomb-bay, crawling between two column supports, before turning around and rising from his stooped position to stand. There were adjustable footrests to enable him to position his head and eyes directly behind the optic head of the Sperry K-3 computing sight, and he had the option of standing or sitting on a seat by means of hooking on a strap which was also adjustable through a belt and buckle.

Regardless of whether the gunner chose to sit or stand, the clutches and controls were close at hand. Toggle switches opened and closed the main power circuits. The main circuit breaker was on a junction box near the gunner's left shoulder, along with the plug-in panel for his heated suit, a light, and the circuit breaker for the K-3 gunsight. The azimuth clutch was a small crank or lever located just above the left ammunition can, while the elevation clutch was above the right ammunition can.

The K-3 sight, which was held upright in a mounting bracket on the sight cradle by a long mounting pin, automatically computed the lead and ballistics as the gunner tracked a target. Three flexible shafts connected to the sight carried the turret movement and range data which the sight needed for computing deflections. Gunners were instructed not to operate the turret under power unless the sight was switched on, as it would have suffered from excessive wear. In order to move the turret, gunners were instructed to:

SPERRY A-1 TOP TURRET

With Me 163 attacks almost always coming from above due to the *Komet*'s method of operation, the most advantageous position for defense against it was the upper/top turret. The B-17G was fitted with a powered Sperry A-1 (or slightly improved A-1-A) upper, or top turret. It was located in the upper section of the fuselage, just behind the pilot's compartment, and its role was to defend the whole top area of the aircraft. The turret was installed with two 0.50-cal. Browning M2 machine guns, and was operated hydraulically on pressure built up by a constant speed electric motor. It was able to turn 360 degrees in azimuth (6,400 mils). In elevation, the guns could be lowered and raised from a little below the horizontal (-5 degrees) to almost straight upwards (85 degrees – 1,509 mils).

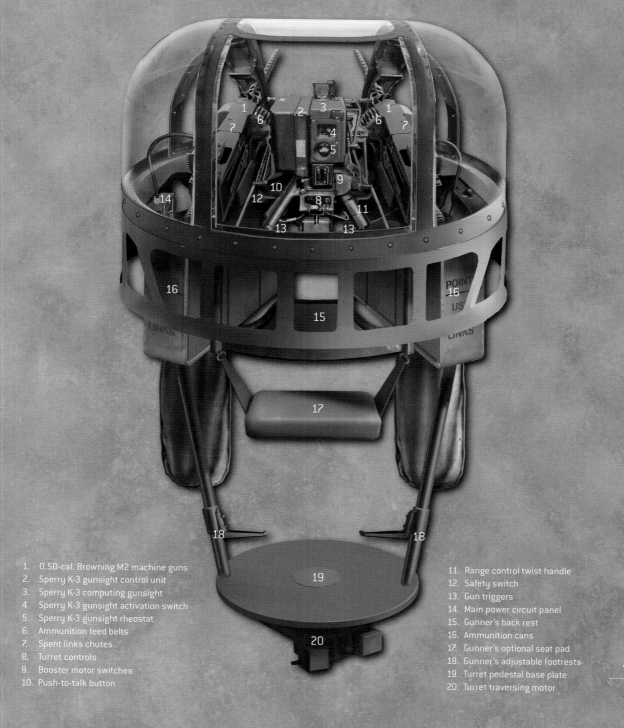

1. 0.50-cal. Browning M2 machine guns
2. Sperry K-3 gunsight control unit
3. Sperry K-3 computing gunsight
4. Sperry K-3 gunsight activation switch
5. Sperry K-3 gunsight rheostat
6. Ammunition feed belts
7. Spent links chutes
8. Turret controls
9. Booster motor switches
10. Push-to-talk button
11. Range control twist handle
12. Safety switch
13. Gun triggers
14. Main power circuit panel
15. Gunner's back rest
16. Ammunition cans
17. Gunner's optional seat pad
18. Gunner's adjustable footrests
19. Turret pedestal base plate
20. Turret traversing motor

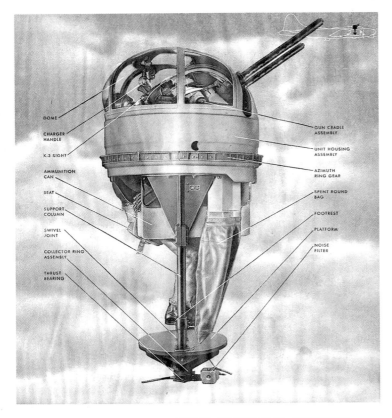

Labels (clockwise from upper left):
DOME
CHARGER HANDLE
K-3 SIGHT
AMMUNITION CAN
SEAT
SUPPORT COLUMN
SWIVEL JOINT
COLLECTOR RING ASSEMBLY
THRUST BEARING
GUN CRADLE ASSEMBLY
UNIT HOUSING ASSEMBLY
AZIMUTH RING GEAR
SPENT ROUND BAG
FOOTREST
PLATFORM
NOISE FILTER

THE SPERRY UPPER

The Sperry Upper Turret is the upstairs brother of the Sperry Ball. It is mounted in the B-17, in the upper portion of the fuselage just behind the pilot's compartment. Its job is to defend the whole top area of the plane.

The "upstairs brother" – a schematic of the B-17's Sperry A-1 upper turret as contained in the May 1944 issue of the USAAF's "Gunner's Information File – Flexible Gunnery," published by the Training Aids Division in the Office of the Assistant Chief of Air Staff, Training Headquarters. (Author's Collection)

Turn the handles just as you would steer a bicycle – to the right to go right, left to go left. Press down on the heels of the handles to raise the guns. Pull up on them to lower the guns. Don't jerk the controls. Move them smoothly. The smoother your tracking, the better your aim with the automatic sight.

On the right handle was a motorcycle handgrip used as a range control knob, which the gunner turned to keep the sight reticles framing the target. Next to his thumb on the left handle was the push-to-talk button which opened the interphone system. The interphone jacks for connecting the headphones and throat microphone led out of the junction box by the gunner's left shoulder. Under the index fingers were the triggers. Charger handles were suspended from pulleys on the turret dome. To charge the guns, the gunner grasped the handles and pulled them down as sharply as he could, before allowing the handles to go back under their own power, while keeping his hands on the handles.

There was a demand-type oxygen regulator with hose mask connection directly in front of the gunner below the control unit, while close to his right shoulder was the oxygen flow (which came from the bomber's central tanks) and pressure gauge.

Just prior to a mission, the gunner would clean the Plexiglas panels of the turret dome, check the alignment of the guns and the sight by boresighting, check that the hydraulic breather caps were one-quarter full with fluid, and that the power clutches were engaged and the hand cranks disengaged. He would then load the ammunition boxes and feed the ammunition to the guns. All hydraulic units and sights had to be warmed up at least five minutes before take-off. Then he would check the response of the azimuth and elevation mechanisms by manipulating the hand control unit, turn the range adjuster and check that the reticles moved in response and, finally, adjust the reticle light to the desired brilliance.

Just before take-off, the gunner pressed the ammunition belts into the guns' feedways over the belt holding pawl. When in flight, he would charge both guns on order from the flight commander.

COMBAT

Pressing on with its campaign against enemy oil targets, during the morning of July 28, 1944, in inclement weather, as the Allied armies in Normandy broke out of the Cherbourg Peninsula, the Eighth Air Force sent a strong force of 688 B-17s from 18 combat wings to strike at Leuna and Leipzig. The Fifteenth Air Force, flying from airfields in Italy, bombed the Ploesti oil refineries in Rumania. The Third Reich was effectively and increasingly under siege.

In response to the raid on Leuna, the Luftwaffe sent up 131 single-engined fighters and 40 *Zerstörer*, of which only 40 of the former made contact with the bombers. From Brandis, 1./JG 400 scrambled seven Me 163s as the B-17s of the 1st and 3rd BDs approached the Leuna complex. However, over the target area, the P-38 and P-51 fighter escorts managed to keep the small number of rocket fighters at bay, and they apparently made no attempt to attack the bombers.

The presence of the Me 163s was described in the Eighth Air Force's subsequent INTOPS summary for the mission as being "a most interesting development." The bomber crews reported observing the interceptors diving between their formations, and although they did not attack, they were described as "highly maneuverable but unstable, yet faster, especially in a steep climb, than the P-51s which pursued them."

This was borne out by Col Avelin P. Tacon Jr., commander of the 359th Fighter Group (FG), whose P-51s were escorting the B-17s as they completed their bombing run over Merseburg-Leuna. One of the fighter group's pilots had called in contact with the rocket fighters after sighting contrails about 7,000ft above and five miles away from the Mustangs. Tacon reported:

I immediately called them out as jet-propelled aircraft. There was no mistaking their contrails. It was white and very dense – as dense as a cumulus cloud, and the same

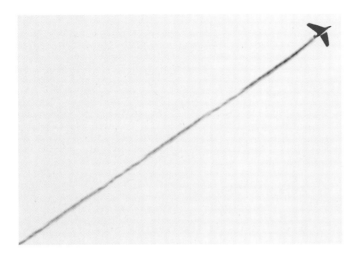

appearance, except it was elongated. The two contrails I saw were about three-fourths of a mile long.

Tacon ordered his flight to drop their tanks, and they went in pursuit of the enemy aircraft, trying to make a head-on, overhead pass:

Their rate of roll appeared to be excellent, but radius of turn very large. I estimate, conservatively, they were doing between 500–600mph. Although I had seen them start their dive and watched them throughout their attack, I had no time to get my sights anywhere near them. Both ships, still in close formation and without jet propulsion, passed about 1,000ft under us.

Tacon split-essed to try to catch the *Komets*:

As soon as they had passed under us, one of them continued on in a 45-degree dive and the other pulled up into the sun, which was about 50 or 60 degrees above the horizon. I glanced quickly up into the sun, but could not see this one. When I looked back at the one that had continued the dive, approximately a second later, he was about five miles away down to perhaps 10,000ft. Although I did not see it, the leader of my second flight reports that the aircraft that pulled up into the sun used his jet in short bursts. The flight leader described it as looking like he was blowing smoke rings. This ship disappeared, and we don't know where he went.

While still about 3,000 yards from the bombers, they turned into us and left the bombers alone. In this turn they banked about 80 degrees, but their course changed only

An Me 163B is towed by a three-wheeled *Scheuch-Schlepper* (tug tractor) across the grass following its landing. The tug was powered by a Volkswagen engine, while the tracked trailer operated like a fork-lift, raising an Me 163 high enough to be able to reattach the undercarriage dolly or transport the aircraft supported between its forks. (EN Archive)

about 20 degrees. Their turn radius was very large, but their rate of roll appeared excellent. Their speed I estimated was 500–600mph. Both planes passed under us, 1,000ft below, while still in a close formation glide. In an attempt to follow them, I split-S'd. One continued down in a 45-degree dive, the other climbed up into the sun very steeply and I lost him. Then I looked back at the one in a dive and saw he was five miles away at 10,000ft.

By this time, the sole tactical purpose of the Me 163 was recognized as being an *Objektschütz-Jäger* (Target [or Point] Interceptor), a role which saw it defending a single, assigned target against enemy bombardment. However, it is likely that in these early encounters, the pilots of JG 400 were airborne primarily to try out tactics and cannon, since they avoided making attacks.

Over the coming months, the combat "tactic" generally used by the Me 163 *Staffeln* was simple, being dictated by the aircraft's inherent speed and extreme fuel consumption. After take-off, an Me 163B would climb at speeds reaching 800km/h to an altitude of around 12,000m until its fuel was exhausted. An attack against enemy bombers was made, in some cases, while the aircraft still had fuel, or after it had been expended and during its return dive to the ground. But even after the consumption of its fuel, the rocket interceptor was still fast and maneuverable.

As testimony to this, according to an Allied intelligence report, on one occasion an Me 163, its fuel consumed, was caught at 8,300m by five P-51s. The American fighters attempted to attack the Messerschmitt for 20 minutes before the interceptor pilot was able to evade and get his aircraft down for a safe landing.

On August 16, a massive armada of 1,090 bombers set out to hit a range of oil, aircraft industry, and airfield targets. Some 88 B-17s of the 1st BD struck at Braunkohle-Benzin AG's plant at Böhlen, 101 Flying Fortresses of the 3rd BD bombed the same organization's facility at Zeitz, and 105 B-17s from the same division went to Deutsche Petroleum AG's refinery at Rositz. Additionally, a force of 87 B-24s from the 2nd BD attacked Braunkohle-Benzin AG at Magdeburg-Rothensee.

2Lt Donald M. Waltz, the pilot of B-17G 43-38085 *Towering Titan* of the 365th BS/305th BG, recalled the mission:

I was a Second Lieutenant B-17 pilot in the 365th BS of the 305th BG based at Chelveston [in Northamptonshire]. In the morning my crew and I were briefed for a daylight mission to bomb a German synthetic oil factory southwest of the city of Leipzig. It was only our fourth combat mission. This was considered a deep penetration mission because of Leipzig's location in Germany. We carried the maximum gross weight of fuel and bombs. Our 12-plane squadron was divided into three four-plane elements. I was assigned to

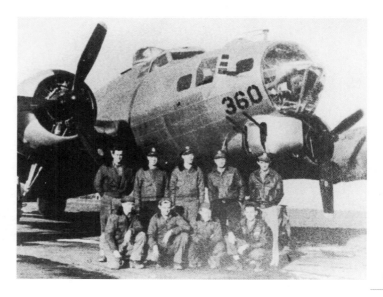

The crew of B-17G 43-38085 *Towering Titan* of the 365th BS/ 305th BG had a lucky escape on August 16, 1944 when Feldwebel Herbert Straznicky of 1./JG 400 attacked them from "six o'clock high" in a steep dive. Sgt Howard J. Kaysen, the tail gunner "plastered" Straznicky's Me 163 and the interceptor dived away and crashed. 2Lt Don Waltz, pilot, is seen here standing second from left, while Kaysen is in the front row, third from left. (Don Waltz)

The standard USAAF Combat Wing formation fielded 54 B-17s (sometimes mixed with B-24s) in three "boxes" of bombers (in High, Lead, and Low positions), each consisting of three six-aircraft squadrons echeloned into Lead, High, and Low. In turn, the squadrons were formed of two three-aircraft flights (High and Low). Such a formation, despite requiring considerable assembly time and disciplined flight control, ensured a high level of mutual protection and defense, although the bombers flying in the second flights of the Low squadrons were most vulnerable – they were a favorite target for rear-mounted attacks by German interceptors, including Me 163s. Nevertheless, attacking such a formation – even without the presence of a strong fighter escort – was a daunting prospect.

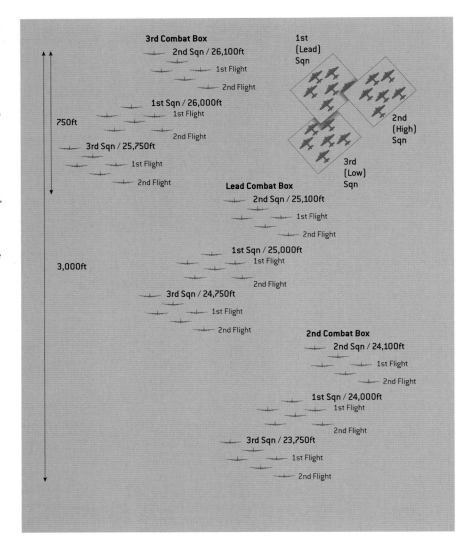

fly off squadron leader Lt W. E. Jenks' left wing in the four-ship lead element. I think 2Lt Charles Laverdiere was assigned the slot position.

Our Bomb Group had been briefed for the previous ten days on the possibility of attack by a new German "jet" fighter plane, the Me 163. At our early morning briefing on August 16, our Group Intelligence Officer again described the Me 163. He said the airplane was in early production – not too many in operation, so we were "unlikely to see the Me 163 on this Leipzig mission." He further indicated that if we did encounter the Me 163, we would have no problem with aircraft recognition – "it will be the fastest aircraft any of us have seen." I recall that mission being long and rough.

The bombers came with more than 600 escort fighters, almost swamping the defense, which managed to direct 77 piston-engined fighters at the bomber streams.

At Brandis, the fighter controllers once again waited until the bombers were virtually over the airfield before issuing the *Start* order. Yet while Brandis was well located to intercept attacks on the oil plants, in terms of infrastructure, it was proving less than ideal. In reality, the field was too short, the volatile fuel for the Me 163 had to be stored on the surface in rail tanker wagons, and repair facilities were lacking.

On the 16th, just five Me 163s were operationally ready, and they took off in quick succession, climbing sharply and fast. By late morning, as the 1st BD neared Böhlen, the rocket interceptors headed down toward the lead element of B-17s from the 365th BS, sweeping through the formation. The first to go in was the *Komet* flown by Feldwebel Herbert Straznicky, who dived 600m from "six o'clock high" toward 2Lt Waltz's *Towering Titan*. Manning the tail gun position was Sgt Howard J. Kaysen, known as "Red" to his fellow crew. He opened fire on the Messerschmitt at 1,000 yards, but Straznicky leveled out and closed in to just 50 yards. *Towering Titan*'s navigator was 2Lt Paul Davidson, who later recalled:

"Red" was our best gunner. The Me 163 came within 50 yards and then peeled off as "Red" plastered him. The Me 163 went into a dive trailing black smoke.

As Straznicky's stricken Me 163 fell earthward, the German pilot was able to bail out. He came down safely not far from Brandis airfield, and his aircraft exploded on impact with the ground. Metal splinters had embedded themselves in his left arm and thigh, but he recovered and returned to operations.

A second *Komet* closed in from "six o'clock high" on B-17G XK-G (serial unknown) flown by 1Lt Warren E. Jenks, who was leading the 365th BS that day. Through the Plexiglas dome of the top turret, gunner TSgt H. K. Tubbs opened fire at 800 yards, watching the enemy interceptor speeding in to 200 yards before it

Viennese by birth, 22-year-old Feldwebel Herbert "Niki" Straznicky of 1./JG 400 was a potent Me 163 pilot. He was posted missing following aerial combat on November 2, 1944 and later found dead 12km west of Delitzsch. (Ransom Collection)

broke away below the B-17. Other than being subjected to this fruitless attack, Jenks' bomber remained unscathed.

It would be a different story for two other bombers attacked by 28-year-old Leutnant Hartmut "Bubi" Ryll. A combat-seasoned fighter pilot who had joined 1./ JG 400 from 2./JG 77, Ryll had been assigned for "jet fighter" training in October 1943. Flying Bf 109Gs over Italy, he had been credited with

Smiling for the camera, Leutnant Hartmut Ryll of 1./JG 400 prepares to jump down from the cockpit of his Me 163. A Berliner by birth and a determined rocket pilot, he was shot down and killed by P-51s on August 16, 1944 after mounting an attack on B-17s. (Ransom Collection)

six victories, his last being a P-38 shot down on August 30, 1943 over the Mediterranean coast between Rome and Naples.

According to Späte, Ryll had attempted to engage B-17s on July 28 and 29, but on both occasions he had been unsuccessful. His tactical method was to attack a bomber in a vertical dive, even when he risked being pursued by an escort fighter. Ryll recounted:

If you go into a vertical dive, the aircraft following you will fire his munitions over you! The guns in a fighter aircraft are harmonized for horizontal flight. The guns are adjusted up so that the trajectory of the shells will follow a ballistic curve to compensate for the pull of gravity. Therefore, the enemy has too much lead since there is no longer any deflection of the trajectory caused by the gravitational pull of the earth.

Naturally, you have to keep your nerve, keep the aeroplane in a vertical dive, and then, with your chin tucked in for support, pull hard to level out. And by the time the airspeed dissipates from 900km/h, you're already back in the local area and under the protection of our own Flak.

Ryll fell upon the B-17 flown by 2Lt Charles Laverdiere, closing in with such speed that the startled tail gunner bailed out. Ryll was very aggressive and accurate in his attack, the fire from his two 30mm cannon killing one of the gunners, striking both of the B-17's inboard engines, shooting up the flaps, and damaging the tail. But that was not enough for Ryll, who climbed and turned in again from "two o'clock" for a second pass, during which he hit the ball turret, its gunner literally being shot out into the sky. Somehow, Laverdiere managed to fly the damaged bomber back to base, where he later told intelligence officers how his aircraft had been shot up by a heavily armed "bat-shaped" aircraft which was so fast that his gunners were unable to track it.

After damaging Laverdiere's B-17, Ryll went for another as he passed through the enemy formation. This time he made for a "straggler" from the lead squadron of the 91st BG, based at Bassingbourn, in Cambridgeshire, and one of the component groups of the 1st Combat Wing of the 1st BD.

This Flying Fortress had endured a particularly heavy earlier attack from a pair of Bf 109s from JG 3 and an Fw 190 of IV.(*Sturm*)/JG 3 while on its inward route passing over the town of Eisenach. The German fighters had knocked out the superchargers in the bomber's Nos. 3 and 4 engines, and also damaged the No. 2 engine. This meant the aircraft had less than half of its normal power. The tail gunner had been left badly wounded in his right leg and the top turret gunner had received a head wound, albeit more superficial. The pilot, 1Lt Reese Walker "Moon" Mullins from Covington, Tennessee, ordered his bombardier to jettison the bombs to lighten the aircraft, but he determined to fly on with just one-and-a-half engines, alone, below and some way north of the main 91st BG formation.

There has been some debate about the identity of this aircraft, it being generally considered that the bomber was B-17G 42-31636 *OUT HOUSE MOUSE* of the 323rd BS, although another source has maintained it was B-17G 42-31579 *Betty Lou's Buggy* of the 324th BS. In one interview, however, Mullins stated he was flying the former aircraft when, at 1045 hrs, Hartmut Ryll climbed up to around 18,000m, his Me 163 trailing white vapor, before banking over and coming in from "six o'clock", gliding, as his fuel was expended, and firing his cannon all the way. "Here he comes," called in gunner Sgt Robert D. Loomis from the waist hatch.

Mullins immediately started to rock the B-17 up and down, before, according to co-pilot, 2Lt Franklin P. Drewery from Franklin, Virginia, "skidding back and forth" in an attempt at evasive action. "The 'Jettie' looked like a bat," Mullins said in a subsequent newspaper interview. "Its fuselage was a minor part, for it was practically all wings. When it made a vertical climb at high speed, it left a vapor trail. After gaining altitude above us, the pilot seemed to shut off the power, for no vapor trail was seen." For all his aggression, Ryll did not succeed in hitting the damaged bomber, for as Loomis recounted, "This 'Jettie' couldn't get his guns trained on us."

According to the crew's statements, after his firing pass, Ryll banked to the right and glided on a parallel course to the B-17, but just out of range of its guns. The ball turret gunner, SSgt Kenneth J. Blackburn, asked Mullins to dip the left wing so that he could attempt a burst from his twin Brownings, but just at that moment Flt Off O. V. Chaney, the bombardier, who was standing in for the wounded top turret gunner, told him to hold fire as he had spotted a P-51 diving on the Me 163.

Indeed, help was at hand for the stricken bomber in the shape of a pair of P-51s of the 359th FG flown by Lt Col John B. Murphy and his wingman, 1Lt Cyril W. Jones.

The Mustangs were flying over Bad Lausick, to the southeast of Leipzig, when Murphy had observed what he identified as a vertical, dense, white, non-atmospheric contrail, half-a-mile in length, heading towards the last "box" of bombers. Murphy concluded that it must be from one of the new German "jet" fighters which had been reported by USAAF Intelligence, but he also knew it would be impossible for the Mustangs to catch the aircraft from where they were.

A few moments later, he spotted a straggling B-17 some two miles away to his right. Instinctively, he and Jones veered off towards the vulnerable

This close-up of the nose of B-17G 42-31636 *OUT HOUSE MOUSE* of the 323rd BS/91st BG at Bassingbourn shows to advantage the port side nose gun and the Bendix "chin" turret, with its two 0.50-cal. Browning M2 machine guns. (Ransom Collection)

ENGAGING THE ENEMY

At a speed in excess of 650km/h, the pilot of an Me 163B from JG 400 aims his rocket interceptor at the rear of a formation of B-17s. The "tactics" used by JG 400 were variable, sometimes extemporary, and dictated by the aircraft's high speed and limited endurance. However, approach was usually made by climbing sharply at full speed to the side and above an enemy formation before the pilot dived down toward it, making a single firing pass with his 30mm MK 108 cannon and then hastily exiting, after which the Walter HWK 109-509-A-1 rocket motor would cut out and the pilot would descend in a glide.

The pilot's left hand holds the throttle lever, while his right pushes the KG 12E control column, with his thumb on the firing button for the two 30mm MK 108 wing-mounted cannon.

The Revi 16B gunsight is seen mounted to the top of the instrument panel. This sight required the pilot to estimate the angle of deflection to the target according to combat conditions, but in reality, this could only be done with any degree of accuracy when engaging at short range and/or when attacking from a central position with minimum deflection.

When not required, the gunsight could be collapsed or folded away to one side. The Revi 16B incorporated a sun visor, night vision filter, light bulb, and dimmer switch.

straggler to offer it protection, keeping an eye on the contrail, and as they arrived, Ryll was just leveling out following his attack on Mullins' B-17. The two P-51 pilots gave chase, and Murphy began to overtake, probably because the now fuelless Me 163 was gliding with declining speed. Murphy reported:

As I closed on him, I opened fire from about 1,000ft and held it until I overshot. I scored a few hits on the left side of the fuselage. I pulled up to the left as sharply as I could to prevent overshooting and getting out in front of him, and lost sight of both him and my wingman. My wingman, Lt Jones, reported that the "jettie" flipped over on his back in a half roll.

Jones reported:

The enemy aircraft that we were trying to intercept completed his run on the formation of bombers, passing through them and heading for the straggler. He completed the run on the straggler, and he passed about 500 yards in front and to starboard of the bomber when we overtook them. White Leader [Murphy] was about 1,000ft ahead of me and about 500ft above me on the final approach. I saw White Leader fire, and strikes appeared on the tail of the enemy aircraft. White Leader broke away, and I continued in, the jet aircraft split-essed, and I followed him. I fired a short burst with a three-radii lead and observed no hits. I increased the lead and fired again. The entire canopy seemed to dissolve on the enemy aircraft, which I had identified as an Me 163. I closed very fast and broke behind him.

As I passed behind the enemy aircraft, I hit his wash and did a half-turn. While recovering, I blacked out and lost sight of the Me 163. I recovered at 14,000ft after

The crew of B-17G 42-31636 *OUT HOUSE MOUSE* of the 323rd BS/91st BG, photographed at their Bassingbourn home. Kneeling, from left to right, are TSgt James R. Knaub (radio operator), SSgt Kenneth J. Blackburn (ball-turret gunner), Sgt Joe V. Cullen (assistant engineer and waist gunner), SSgt Robert D. Loomis (armorer and waist gunner), Sgt Gordon D. Smith (tail gunner, replaced on August 16 mission by SSgt M. D. Baker), and TSgt Carl A. Dickson (engineer and top turret gunner). Standing, from left to right, are Flt Off Raymond Nassimbent (co-pilot, replaced on August 16 mission by 2Lt Forest P. Drewery), 1Lt W. Reese "Moon" Mullins (pilot), 2Lt John O'Connor (navigator and nose gunner), and Flt Off O. V. Chanes (bombardier and chin turret gunner). (Ransom Collection)

Me 163B-1 CANNON ARMAMENT

After an initial fitment of two 20mm MG 151/20 cannon, standard armament on the Me 163B-1 operational aircraft settled on two 30mm MK 108 cannon, which were known to be very effective against Allied heavy bombers. The weapons were installed in the wing roots, and unlike the MG 151, they were located a little higher and slightly further outboard. The shorter barrel of the MK 108 meant that the weapon did not protrude from the wing leading edge, unlike the MG 151. However, because of the flight characteristics of the Me 163 and its limited ammunition capacity, firing at ranges beyond 400m was considered inefficient.

1. 30mm ammunition round
2. Rheinmetall-Borsig MK 108 cannon
3. Port ammunition feed bin
4. Starboard ammunition feed bin
5. Spent shell ejection chute

starting the attack at 23,000ft. The pilot was surely killed when the bullets entered his canopy, and I claim one Me 163 destroyed. I could not find my leader and being low on gas, I returned home.

For his part, Murphy had climbed and turned sharply to port, at which point he thought he had seen another Me 163. This aircraft, however, was probably still Ryll, who was now in a shallow dive. Murphy throttled back so that he did not overtake the *Komet*, firing a "continuous burst" at his target. He saw:

> Continuous strikes the full length of the fuselage. Parts began falling off, followed by a big explosion and more parts falling off. I could smell strange chemical fumes in my cockpit as I followed through the smoke from the explosion. It seemed to me that a large chunk of the fuselage from the canopy on back just popped off with the explosion.

The fumes which Murphy noticed may well have been caused by the Me 163's burning fuel. He claimed one Me 163 destroyed and one damaged. In fact, he and Jones had shared in the destruction of Ryll's aircraft, an early Me 163B, which crashed vertically into the ground west of Brandis at 1052 hrs, a tall column of smoke emitting from the wreckage. Ryll was killed – upon the recovery of his body, it was found he had suffered fatal head and chest wounds prior to impact.

Clearly, the speed of the Me 163 had initially shocked the American pilots, Murphy commenting:

My first impression when I saw the jet-plane was that I was standing still. It seemed hopeless to try to attempt to overtake it, but my actions were prompted by a curiosity to get as close to it as possible. I believe that will be the reaction of every pilot that comes in contact with one. Another thing that is very noticeable is that the jet-plane's speed varies considerably, but it's hard to realize this until you find yourself rapidly overtaking one.

Jones echoed Lt Col Murphy's sentiments:

While the Me 163 has his jet in operation, it would be impossible for the P-51 to overtake it, but with the jet off or expended, it seems to be slower than the P-51. It is difficult to judge the speed of the jet aircraft with its power off, and its speed seems to change very quickly. I had no chance to maneuver with the Me 163 beyond my firing point, and could not very well determine its maneuverability. It climbs at an almost vertical angle, faster than the conventional aircraft can cruise in level flight; that is, with its power on. It also has very great acceleration with its power on, and a fast gliding speed immediately after using its power.

The small number of Me 163s from 1./JG 400 had been in action for 15 minutes. In that time, Leutnant Hartmut Ryll had been lost and Feldwebel Herbert Straznicky wounded. On the plus side, it is believed that Feldwebel Friedrich Schubert, a man described by Späte as "a calm and passive individual on the ground," accounted for a B-17 shot down with just three bursts fired from his MK 108 cannon.

A subsequent USAAF report noted of the action on August 16:

The gunners of the bomber formation stated that the enemy aircraft were so fast that it was impossible to track them with turrets or free guns. Speed was in excess of that of an escort fighter diving at 400mph ASI [airspeed indicator] [595mph true airspeed] at 25,000ft, although at one time the speed of the enemy aircraft when flying straight and level was estimated to be as low as 150mph.

As for Mullins and his crew, and their battered B-17, miraculously, they made it back home.

If the Allies had anything to do with it, the Me 163s would be kept busy in their aerial defense of the refineries. Less than a week after JG 400's clash with the 1st BD around Böhlen and Leipzig, in a report of August 21, the Joint Intelligence Committee claimed that every hydrogenation plant in Germany had been damaged by bombing, and also that five of the Fischer-Tropsch plants had been damaged. This served to generate ever more enthusiasm for the continuation of the oil offensive amongst the Allies – the British were especially enthused, and suggested "serious consideration should

Four Me 163Bs on the rain-wet concrete at Brandis in August or September 1944. The aircraft are covered with protective tarpaulins, and generator starter carts are at readiness, as are access ladders for the pilots to enter the cockpits. (EN Archive)

be given to according overall priority to the attack of oil targets by the Allied Strategic Bomber Forces," including RAF Bomber Command raids on oil targets in the Ruhr.

Meanwhile, on August 20, 1./JG 400 reported 14 Me 163s available, of which five were serviceable. By then, a *Stab* I./JG 400 was forming up to be based at Brandis, while 1.*Staffel* was complete and fully deployed. 2./JG 400, based at Venlo, in the Netherlands, close to the German border and ideally located for the defense of the Ruhr plants, had also completed formation with personnel and eight Me 163Bs. Planned 3., 4., 5., and 6.*Staffeln* and an *Ergänzungsstaffel* were at various stages of establishment and training.

Four days later, on the 24th, the USAAF launched one of the largest raids of the war against the refineries and synthetic oil and aircraft plants. The mission again saw joint operations by the Eighth and Fifteenth Air Forces, with the former despatching 1,300 bombers to targets including Leuna, Ruhland, Brüx, Misburg, and Freital, while 600 aircraft from the Fifteenth targeted oil refineries in western Germany and Czechoslovakia. In addition, no fewer than 626 fighters were active over occupied Europe, protecting the Eighth's bombers. The Luftwaffe reaction was described as "generally slight and ineffective," with I.*Jagdkorps* compelled to divide its forces to deploy against both USAAF air forces. It is believed only 99 Luftwaffe fighters made contact.

At Brandis, again the small number of Me 163s was scrambled to intercept. Leutnant Hans Bott had only recently joined 1./JG 400, having previously served as an instructor with *Flugzeugführerschule* A/B 10 at Warnemünde and then JG 104. He remembered:

On August 24, 1944 there were eight Me 163s available for seven operational pilots. My first combat sortie should have taken place a few days earlier, but on that occasion I had experienced my first engine flame-out. I climbed to a high altitude and we suddenly saw below us, to port, a formation of B-17 bombers flying at a height of about 9,000m. I dived without power – I had already shut down the engine on leveling out – in order to get behind the bombers but, after completing the dive, I was relieved to find that I could no longer see them. I landed, but then felt an unaccountable rage well up. On landing I saw the eighth aircraft, and told my driver to take me to it. I recognized the aircraft as one that I had flown previously, because it was the only one armed with two MG 151 machine guns.

High above, the 305th BG was flying as part of the 1st BD, targeting Leuna that day. Piloting 364th BS B-17G *SPARE PARTS* (serial unknown) was 2Lt Eugene Arnold Jr. He recalled:

Our mission was to Merseburg, Germany, to bomb the Leuna synthetic oil works. Merseburg was a tough target because it was deep inside Germany (a ten-hour raid) and it was protected by anti-aircraft guns lined up along our bombing run. While flying deep in Germany, we were startled to see a very small enemy fighter plane pull right up to our left wingtip and fly formation with us. Our engineer, Tony Lanzano, yelled over the intercom, "Hey, Arnold, there's a plane off of our left wing with no propeller!" Sure enough, there did not seem to be anything pulling him through the air. The German pilot and I were staring at each other (we were only 65ft apart). I assumed he was there to observe our formation so the Germans could more effectively attack us with their fighters.

I told the gunners to fire at him (even my guys couldn't miss at that range), and as he saw our turrets move, he flipped up his right wing so that his heavily armored belly was exposed and he shot ahead of us with a speed none of us had ever seen in an airplane (we had experience with the V2 rockets swooshing past us at high-altitude, but they were going up and left large contrails).

Meanwhile, Leutnant Hans Bott had climbed into the last flight-ready Me 163 on the ground at Brandis:

I used almost the whole length of the runway to take off, the combustion chamber pressure being too low at 22 atmospheres. The course I had to fly took me towards Leipzig. I encountered a formation of bombers while still climbing and fired at an aircraft on the port side of the formation. As soon as I began firing my MG 151 machine guns [sic], one of them jammed, but the other continued to fire, and I saw my shells hit the aircraft. Using the last of my fuel, I carried on climbing to 9,000m and dived back down at high speed. I was in the air for seven minutes.

It is possible Bott's victim was shot down, with the B-17 probably coming from the 92nd BG. The crews of at least 13 Flying Fortresses claimed to have been attacked by Me 163s over the target area. A second bomber from the 92nd BG is believed to have been badly damaged in an attack by Feldwebel Siegfried Schubert, who is thought to have shot down B-17G 42-97571 from the 750th BS/457th BG. The aircraft, flown by 2Lt Winfred Pugh, was flying in the No. 3 position in the lead squadron, lead box. According to the subsequent Missing Air Crew Report:

2Lt Eugene Arnold Jr., seen here front row at far left, was the pilot of B-17G SPARE PARTS of the 364th BS/305th BG. His crew flew to Merseburg on August 24, and Arnold described it as a "tough target." Alerted by engineer TSgt Tony Lanzano (rear row at far right), SPARE PARTS was approached by an Me 163 that closed in to just 65ft on the port side. The bomber's gunners opened fire and the interceptor pulled away. (Author's Collection)

B-17G FLYING FORTRESS

Cheyenne-built B-17G-25-BO 42-31713 *SNAKE HIPS* was flown by 2Lt John Bosko, and crew, of the 327th BS/ 92nd BG in August 1944. This aircraft was delivered to the USAAF on December 10, 1943 and assigned to the 327th BS at Podington, in Bedfordshire, on February 11, 1944. 42-31713 is typical of the B-17Gs that took part in the offensive against the oil plants. It was badly damaged by Flak during the mission to Merseburg on August 24, when a number of bombers were engaged by *Komets*, but the aircraft made it back to base. The 1st BD, which was assigned Merseburg (and others) as a target that day, lost 16 B-17s to enemy action.

OPPOSITE

This diagram shows how an Me 163 pilot would typically engage an approaching Allied bomber formation.

The B-17 made an apparently normal peel-off from the formation at altitude 15,000ft, time 1212 hrs, lost 200ft of altitude and spiraled down. Soon after leaving the formation, one body was seen leaving the aircraft through the escape hatch. The plane spiraled twice, whipped up into a stall, and then spun toward the ground. It exploded between 5,000–10,000ft and three or four chutes were seen. One observer noted a large fire in the left wing [and] another observer believed the Nos. 2 and 3 engines were on fire. The wings were believed to have been blown off in the explosion.

As Späte wrote in his memoirs of this mission, "The ice appeared to be broken."

After *SPARE PARTS* landed back at Chelveston, 2Lt Arnold met with an intelligence officer, to whom he recounted seeing "a fast plane that did not have a propeller." The intelligence officer enquired of the bomber pilot how many drinks he had had.

Somewhat tardily, on September 8, the *General der Jagdflieger*, Generalmajor Adolf Galland, declared the Me 163 operational:

The port wing between the engines of a B-17 bursts into flames as it is struck by cannon rounds fired from an Me 163. It is possible that this *Komet* was being flown by Feldwebel Friedrich Schubert of 1./JG 400 on August 24, 1944, and that the Flying Fortress is "straggler" 42-97571 from the 750th BS/457th BG with 2Lt Winfred Pugh at the controls. (Ransom Collection)

Me 163 Target Defense Tactics

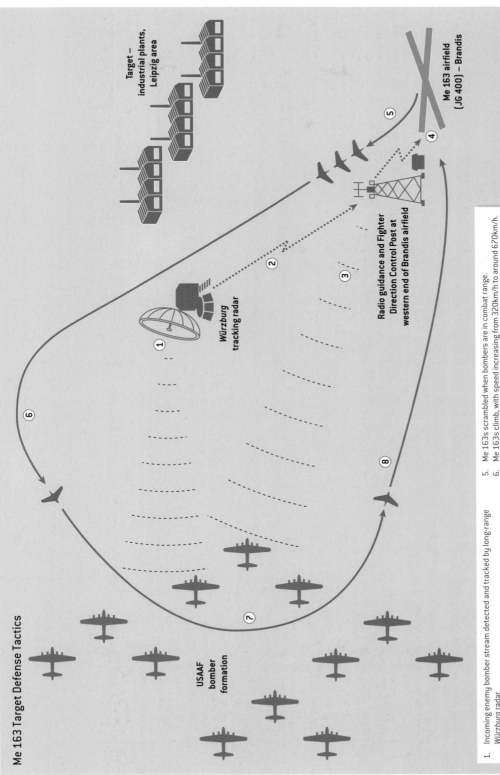

Target – industrial plants, Leipzig area

Me 163 airfield (JG 400) – Brandis

Radio guidance and Fighter Direction Control Post at western end of Brandis airfield

Würzburg tracking radar

USAAF bomber formation

1. Incoming enemy bomber stream detected and tracked by long-range *Würzburg* radar.
2. Course and estimated strength of enemy bomber stream relayed to Fighter Direction Control Post.
3. Fighter Direction Control Post plots track of bomber stream as it enters operational radius of Brandis-based Me 163s.
4. Data on approach of bombers relayed to airfield where Me 163s are at readiness.
5. Me 163s scrambled when bombers are in combat range.
6. Me 163s climb, with speed increasing from 320km/h to around 670km/h. Upon sighting enemy bombers, speed could increase to around 850km/h. Me 163 could climb to up to 12,000m in as little as three minutes. Me 163 dives at angle of 45 degrees to make attack.
7. Me 163 passes through bomber formation, making cannon attack.
8. Me 163 returns in glide to base.

The first operational *Staffel* has shot down three four-engined bombers with certainty and two probably, and has confirmed the usefulness of and the tactics envisaged for this aircraft in combat. Measures will be taken to increase the number of each squadron's aircraft and pilots to 20 in order to improve their effectiveness. The aircraft's readiness has been up till now adversely impaired by the lack of spare parts for the airframe and engine.

For the rest of that month, I./JG 400 responded to the further raids against the oil plants by sending up the small numbers of available and operationally ready Me 163s. The rocket interceptors are known to have been active on September 11, 12, 13, and 28, but success eluded the *Komet* pilots. This would change on October 7 – although for I./JG 400, success would come at a high cost.

By this time, the plants at Leuna and Brüx had been correctly identified by the Allies as supplying aviation fuel, and thus they, along with Böhlen, became priority targets in an attempt to curtail Luftwaffe activity.

Around Leipzig, the 7th would see the Eighth Air Force strike at Böhlen, Lützkendorf, and Leuna with forces of 86, 88, and 129 B-17s from the 3rd BD bombing each respective target. At Brandis around 15 to 20 Me 163s had been brought to readiness – Späte described it as "an impressive force!"

The rocket interceptors mounted two attacks. Firstly, on receipt of the *Alarmstart* just before midday, Feldwebel Schubert, accompanied by Leutnante Bott and Rolf Glogner took off, followed by Oberfeldwebel Friedrich-Peter Husser and Unteroffizier Manfred Eisenmann. The Me 163s went straight for the Flying Fortresses of the 95th BG, approaching from various positions. Defensive fire from the bombers damaged the tail of Schubert's aircraft, while Bott, coming up from below, opened fire on a B-17 in the lead flight of the high squadron. His fusillade of cannon fire hit the bomber's right wing. At 1210 hrs, in a head-on attack, Schubert fired a burst at a B-17 that fell away from its formation. Schubert's aircraft was moving so fast there was nothing the P-51 escorts of the 352nd FG could do. Elsewhere, other Me 163s flashed through the bombers, their cannon firing.

2Lt Ralph M. Brown, flying a 95th BG B-17 which, it is believed, Schubert attempted to attack, wrote in his diary:

I had a pilot called Philpott as my co-pilot, and this was his first mission. Since this target was in the Leipzig area, I was expecting a rough trip, and we got it today in the form of Jerry fighters. Just after turning on the IP [Initial Point], we were hit by Me 109s,

2Lt Ralph M. Brown and his crew from the 95th BG experienced an Me 163 attack on October 7, 1944. "They pounded our formation pretty hard in about two passes," he wrote later. Here, 2Lt Brown is seen center, front row. (Author's Collection)

Fw 190s, and the new jet jobs – Me 163s. They pounded our formation pretty hard in about two passes. We were very fortunate as our ship didn't take any hits from the fighters' 20mm [*sic*]. We went on into and off the target safely. When I saw that 20mm bursting in little bright flashes, I sure shoved my wing into the tightest formation I ever flew and thanked my lucky stars. I was flying wing on the lead ship, as that is an easy place to fly. After we got back, Philpott thought it was an easy mission, but since that was his first, I guess he didn't realize how rough it was.

However, things did not start well for I./JG 400's second attack. As Me 163B V61 GN+MD, flown by Schubert, gathered speed in its take-off run in a tailwind some 50m ahead of the *Komet* flown by Bott, the combustion chamber in the fully-fueled aircraft caught fire and the fighter rolled off the runway and somersaulted. The aircraft's thrust axis was below its vertical center of gravity, and this caused it to pitch nose up, turn over, and explode.

Probably in a state of shock, Bott nevertheless continued his take-off, followed by Husser and Eisenmann. Also airborne was former instructor pilot Oberfeldwebel Helmut Reukauf, as well as Oberfeldwebeln Jupp Mühlstroh and Günther Andreas, and Feldwebel Rudolf Zimmermann. Späte recalled:

You could hear the familiar drone of the Walter rocket engine as the pilots of both squadrons fought in the skies to the west of the airfield.

Unteroffizier Kurt Schiebeler, in Me 163B "White 3," took off at 1230 hrs and attacked a formation of ten B-17s flying in a lead position. He claimed a *Herausschuss* (an aircraft forced out of its formation) and returned to Brandis nine minutes later.

Meanwhile, Bott and Zimmermann climbed at 930km/h at an angle of around 60 degrees, heading for the area 50km southeast of Leipzig. Zimmermann soon spotted a lone B-17 below his right wing. He turned, circling to the left, and dived toward the American bomber, which was 1.5km away below him. At that moment Zimmermann's fuel became expended and he entered a glide, firing, and "saw pieces flying off the bomber."

Altogether, it is believed that some ten bombers came under attack from the *Komets*, but the interceptors' return to base was catastrophic. Husser recounted how:

My main desire was to land as quickly as possible before the bombs began to rain down, and in doing so I made a heavy landing. My aircraft bounced 200m into the air and then glided over the perimeter fence, eventually landing in a sand pit, where the *Komet* flipped over onto its back. A soldier called to me, "Get out, it's going to explode!" I, with blood streaming over my face, could not move. Behind me, I could hear the rocket motor still rumbling. I was eventually rescued by Unteroffizier Harald Kuhn from HWK, who smashed the Plexiglas canopy and pulled me out of the cockpit.

Unteroffizier Kurt Schiebeler of 1./JG 400 made several attacks on B-17s between August and November 1944. [Ransom Collection]

RIGHT

An Me 163 banks to starboard as it is caught by the gun camera of a P-51. It is believed that this is the aircraft flown by Oberfeldwebel Friedrich-Peter Husser of 2./JG 400 pursued by 2Lt Willard G. Erfkamp of the 385th FS/364th FG on October 7, 1944. Husser crash-landed, suffering a head wound as a result, and his aircraft was 65 percent damaged. (Ransom Collection)

FAR RIGHT

With his aircraft's engine still powered, the pilot of an Me 163 attempts to evade the P-51D flown by Capt Louis H. Norley, Operations Officer of the 335th FS/4th FG. Norley claimed the destruction of the Me 163 piloted by Oberfeldwebel Jacob Bollenrath, which crashed and exploded close to Zeititz, a village at the eastern end of the runway at Brandis, on November 2, 1944. However, the aircraft seen here in the same mission, although damaged, managed to escape pursuit by the Mustang. (Ransom Collection)

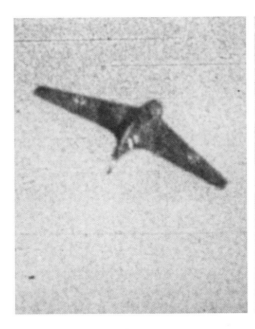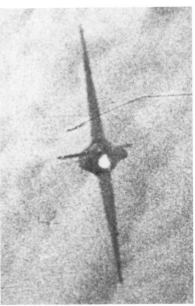

Eisenmann began his approach to land from too great a height. He side-slipped, slammed down hard on the ground, and was catapulted back up into the air. The aircraft performed a number of rolls and then a cartwheel as one of its wingtips hit the ground. The aircraft blew apart and Eisenmann was thrown out of the cockpit, still harnessed to his seat. He suffered a fractured skull and died as a result.

Zimmermann was pursued by P-51s of the 364th FG and bellied into a field at Borna to the south of Leipzig:

Hearing the Mustangs approaching, I jumped out. As the first came in to attack, I ran off at right angles, then dropped down. During several strafing runs my aircraft was shot up like a sieve.

Späte described October 7 as "a terrible day of desperation!"

On November 2 the USAAF again targeted the Leuna hydrogenation plant, deploying 683 bombers from the 3rd BD. Allied commanders were taking no chances, however, and had arranged a fighter screen of 728 P-51s. Leutnant Günter Andreas of 2./JG 400 was assigned to fly one of 17 available Me 163s from Brandis that day. In the early afternoon, after being briefed, the *Komet* pilots of I./JG 400 were taken by lorry to the end of the runway, where they donned their flying suits. After a false start as a result of his mechanic failing to connect his aircraft to the power generator, Andreas' Me 163 whistled into life. He waited patiently while his comrades took off, and then was able to go. He recalled:

After take-off, I immediately turned on to the course given by ground control. During the climb toward Leipzig I saw contrails, and informed ground control that I could proceed on course without further directions. Shortly afterwards, I spotted groups of bombers flying at about 6,000m. I climbed above them to about 10,000m and throttled the engine back to idle to conserve my fuel in case I needed it for an emergency.

Me 163B-0 SG 500 *JÄGERFAUST* ARMAMENT

This artwork shows an Me 163B-0 of 1./JG 400 fitted with 50mm SG 500 *Jägerfaust* four-barrel, single-shot installations. This vertically-firing volley weapon comprised a variable number of rifled tubes that were to be fitted into the wing of an aircraft. Upon the triggering of a photoelectric cell close to a radio aerial near the aircraft's ammunition bay, shells would be fired upwards and into the underside of a bomber as the carrying fighter passed below. The tubes would then be jettisoned downwards. With the 50mm-caliber muzzle velocity of the SG 500 being limited to 400m per second, range to the target had to be reduced to just 50m in order to improve operational efficiency.

At this height, I set course for a tail attack on a B-17 that was flying a little to one side of the main formation of bombers. I opened fire when within range and received, almost instantaneously, return fire from the tail gunner, some of his shells hitting the cockpit. My guns fell silent. The canopy was punctured and I noticed that the armored glass panel in front of me was pockmarked from three of his shells. I was not injured, apart from a small cut over my right eye caused by a fragment from the canopy.

I immediately broke off my attack and attempted to jettison the canopy in case I had to bail out should the aircraft start to burn. At 600km/h the canopy would not budge – it had probably been jammed by the enemy's return fire. I maneuvered to reduce my speed to about 250km/h and then managed, by using my right arm, to release the canopy. Just as the canopy flew off I came under fire from an enemy fighter, and my aircraft, because I had so little speed, nosed over and went into a dive. I attempted to pull out of the dive but realized that the control wires must have been severed in the attack because I could move the control column in all directions without any effect. I decided to bail out, but the first three attempts were unsuccessful because the 163 had begun to dive more steeply, and its drag was too high. I finally bailed out at a height of 5,000–6,000m after the 163 had gained speed and had begun to pull itself out of the dive. I released my parachute and landed in a village close to Wurzen. My aircraft crashed and exploded.

The crew of Lancaster B III ME315 of No. 405 "Vancouver" Sqn which was attacked by the SG 500-equipped Me 163 of Leutnant Friedrich Kelb of 2./JG 400 on April 10, 1945. The pilot, Sqn Ldr Campbell Haliburton Mussells, is fourth from left, while rear gunner, Flt Lt Melborn Mellstrom, who was killed during Kelb's attack, is fifth from left. (Author's Collection)

The shattered rear of ME315, with its missing tail turret, after being hit by a projectile from an SG 500 fired by Leutnant Kelb's Me 163. Sqn Ldr Mussells managed to fly the bomber back to East Anglia, landing at Woodbridge. (Author's Collection)

For I./JG 400, the defensive operations of November 2 saw the loss of Oberfeldwebel Jacob Bollenrath of 1.*Staffel*, who was shot down by a P-51 from the 4th FG. His Me 163B exploded close to the village of Zeititz, near Brandis. Oberfeldwebel Horst Rolly of 2./JG 400 suffered an engine flame-out on take-off. He bailed out of his Me 163B, but his parachute failed to open. Feldwebel Herbert Straznicky of 1.*Staffel* went missing in the Halle-Leipzig area, but was later found dead 12km west of the town of Delitzsch, his Me 163B "White 8" destroyed.

This mission was symptomatic of the punishment the grossly outnumbered Me 163 pilots were absorbing from the fall of 1944, as the Eighth Air Force seemed to field limitless numbers of escort fighters, making the skies over the Reich increasingly dangerous for the Luftwaffe defenders. Indeed, for the pilots of JG 400, the remaining six months of the war were quite desolate, despite the fact that on December 10, 1944, I./JG 400 reported 43 Me 163s on strength, of which 22 were serviceable. Successes became increasingly rare, for getting through the fighters to the bombers was becoming harder, even with the benefit of speed.

There was some cheer on March 16, 1945 when Unteroffizier Rolf Glogner shot down an RAF Mosquito XVI of No. 544 Sqn that was on a photo-reconnaissance sortie over Lützkendorf. "Göring should have awarded me a medal and given me promotion and special leave," Glogner later remarked.

Toward the end of October 1944 Oberst Gordon Gollob, a veteran fighter ace who was overseeing development work on the Me 163, Hauptmann Rudolf Opitz, the acting *Gruppenkommandeur* of I./JG 400, and Hauptmann Anton Thaler, commander of E.Kdo 16, visited Hugo Schneider AG (HASAG) in Leipzig to inspect work on a new 50mm weapon known as the SG 500 *Jägerfaust* (Fighter Fist), and to watch a demonstration. This vertically-firing volley weapon comprised a variable number of rifled firing tubes which were to be fitted into the wing of an aircraft, and upon the triggering of a photoelectric cell (in the development of which HASAG had been engaged), shells would be fired upwards and into the underside of a bomber as the carrying fighter passed below. The tubes would then be jettisoned downwards.

A *Jägerfaust* shell was closed at the bottom, thus forming a cartridge case. The propellant charge and the primer were housed in a paper envelope. The projectile was fed from the muzzle into the rifled section of the tube. Because the 50mm-caliber muzzle velocity of the SG 500 was limited to 400m per second, range to the target was reduced to 50m to improve operational efficiency.

Gollob and Opitz felt the weapon had potential, and subsequently a contract for production was issued, but for installation in the Me 163 the weapon would be adapted to fire 2cm-caliber rounds.

In mid-November 1944 tests were conducted using Me 163B V45 C1+05 of E.Kdo 16, with the photoelectric cell installed close to a radio aerial near the ammunition bay. The SG 500 was first fired against a scrap wing, with no damage being sustained by V45, before Leutnant August Hachtel of the *Kommando* took off on November 13 with half-full fuel tanks and the aircraft's standard MK 108 cannon removed. That test, and subsequent flights, went well, proving the weapon's effectiveness.

Thaler was of the opinion that should the weapon's accuracy prove as good as the theoretical estimates, it would not be necessary to fire all of the shells simultaneously, and he suggested to HASAG that only two or three shells should be fired at the same time, so that two or three bombers could be engaged as an Me 163 passed below. HASAG concurred.

Thaler also suggested that the shells should be capable of being fired by the Me 163 when flying at different speeds. The required switch necessary was already available and had been installed in the aircraft. It allowed the weapon to be fired at any time during three different speed ranges – either when the Me 163 attacked from astern, at one speed range when in a head-on attack, so that it became irrelevant whether the pilot was flying at 700–800km/h or 600–700km/h with thrust, or at 500-600km/h with the engine shut down, or in making a frontal attack. Whatever the case, the switch would prevent the weapon being fired until the aircraft was being flown within the relevant speed range.

It was not until April 10, 1945 that the SG 500 was used in combat. During the early evening, in clear weather, 230 aircraft of RAF Bomber Command attacked the railway yards at Engelsdorf and Mockau in the outer districts of HASAG's base city of Leipzig. At least one Me 163B of 2./JG 400, with Leutnant Friedrich Kelb at the controls, was scrambled from Brandis to intercept them. Kelb was observed to climb sharply above the trees at the end of the runway and then head towards the lead bombers, which were thought to be flying at an altitude of around 8,000m. Such was Kelb's speed and course toward the RAF formation that one observer on the ground viewing events through a long-range Flak telescope feared he would ram one of the bombers.

In fact, Kelb fired his SG 500 at Lancaster B III ME315, a Pathfinder Force bomber flown by Montreal-born Sqn Ldr Campbell Haliburton Mussells of the Royal Canadian Air Force's No. 405 "Vancouver" Sqn as it completed its first pass over the target and was about to commence another. The projectiles from the special weapon shot away the Lancaster's rear gun turret and starboard rudder, shattered the port rudder, and damaged both elevators so badly that they were rendered useless. The rear gunner, Flt Lt Melborn Mellstrom, was in his turret at the time of Kelb's attack and was killed. Damage was also caused to the H2S set and mid-upper turret, the gunner being seriously wounded.

The stricken Lancaster fell 4,000ft, with Mussells having to use all his strength to lash back the control column with a length of rope to keep the nose of the aircraft up. Escorted by P-51s, and with the assistance of his flight engineer, he flew the crippled bomber as far as the British coast, after which he ordered his

OVERLEAF

In the dusk hours of April 10, 1945, a force of 230 aircraft from RAF Bomber Command attacked the Engelsdorf and Mockau railway yards in Leipzig. Within this force were Lancasters of No. 405 "Vancouver" Sqn, the only RCAF unit to serve in the Pathfinder Force. Amongst the aircraft from the squadron involved in the operation was Lancaster B III ME315, flown by Sqn Ldr Campbell Haliburton Mussells. Whilst he orbited his aircraft over the target for a second run, having already released Target Indicator flares, it was attacked by an Me 163 flown by Leutnant Friedrich Kelb of 2./JG 400 that had been scrambled from Brandis to intercept the raid. Kelb's aircraft was fitted with a trial combat installation of the wing-mounted, photo-electrically operated SG 500 *Jägerfaust*.

Kelb approached the bomber formation from behind and above, diving fast into its midst. Once below one of the enemy aircraft, he discharged the SG 500's battery of eight 50mm shells upwards toward Sqn Ldr Mussells' Lancaster. The immediate effect was to blast away the bomber's rear gun turret and its starboard rudder. The Lancaster's rear gunner, Flt Lt Melborn L. Mellstrom, was killed and two other crewmen wounded. Despite its devastating effect, this was the first and only time the SG 500 was used operationally.

The artwork overleaf depicts the moment of the attack as Kelb's Me 163 flashed past below, banking away toward the ground.

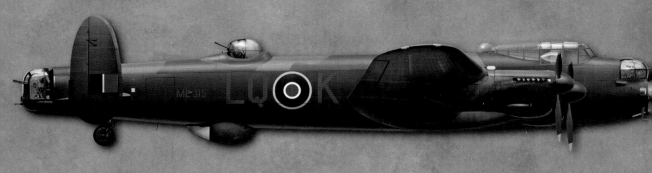

LANCASTER B III

Lancaster B III ME315 of No. 405 "Vancouver" Sqn, as flown by Sqn Ldr Campbell Haliburton Mussells on April 10, 1945 when attacked by an Me 163B flown by Leutnant Friedrich Kelb of 2./JG 400 equipped with a 50mm SG 500 *Jägerfaust* vertically-firing volley weapon. ME315 was built by Avro at Woodford, in Cheshire, in November 1944 and delivered new to No. 7 Sqn at Oakington, in Cambridgeshire. Subsequently passed on to No. 405 Sqn, which was part of RAF Bomber Command's Pathfinder Force, it was repaired after being badly damaged by Kelb's Me 163B. Serving with the RCAF squadron until it disbanded in September 1945, ME315 then spent time with a series of conversion units until the bomber was struck off charge on 19 November 1947 and scrapped.

Leutnant Friedrich Kelb, assigned to 2./JG 400, eases himself into the cockpit of Junkers-built Me 163B Wk-Nr 190579. The identity of the *Komet* fitted with the vertically-firing SG 500 *Jägerfaust* volley weapon is not known. (Ransom Collection)

crew to bail out. Mussels remained with the aircraft and was able land it at Woodbridge, in Suffolk. He was awarded the DSO for his actions during this mission.

Despite his fuel being spent, Kelb was able to evade the Mustang escort and land back at Brandis. It was the first and only time that the SG 500 was known to have been used in combat. The HASAG works were destroyed in the bombing.

With that, effectively, Me 163 successes against Allied bombers had experienced their swansong.

STATISTICS AND ANALYSIS

It is not known exactly how many Allied bombers were shot down by Me 163s, but it is probably less than the number of fingers on both hands. A similar number were probably damaged. Ironically, it was the single most impressive attribute of the Me 163 – its speed – that was also, tactically, its flaw. The aircraft's remarkable speed meant that it took a skilful pilot to close in, aim, open fire, and shoot down a large, self-defended bomber flying in a defensive formation, usually under escort. But this also meant that it was an incredibly difficult target for bomber gunners to track and hit.

It was the opinion of Generalmajor Adolf Galland that the Me 163 was "excellent for point protection of important factories," but that another limiting factor to its capability was the lack of available airfields with the required infrastructure and proximity to industry. Additionally, because of the quick take-offs and landings associated with the aircraft, no more than 20 Me 163s could be based at one airfield.

Again, according to Galland, in terms of tactics, none other than those described in the previous chapter were developed, mainly because of the Me 163's high speed and its short endurance.

It is believed a total of 319 Me 163Bs was delivered, the bulk newly built, but this number also includes some conversions. Of this number, 89 were "held in reserve" by the OKL. As of December 31, 1944, *Stab*, I. and II./JG 400 had 91 aircraft on their combined inventory. Six Me 163s were lost to enemy action and another nine to other causes.

By comparison, some 8,680 B-17G Flying Fortresses were built by Boeing (4,035 aircraft), Douglas (2,395), and Lockheed (Vega) (2,250). Altogether, 12,731 B-17s of all types were constructed between 1935–45.

Shortly after the German surrender, British forces discovered the fuselages of 19 newly completed Junkers-built Me 163Bs, together with disassembled wings and other parts, in storage at a Luftwaffe aircraft park at Kiel-Holtenau. (EN Archive)

The nemesis of the Me 163 was fuel supply. By the fall of 1944, E.Kdo 16 had developed the rocket interceptor to the point where it was ready for operations and *Komet* production had, according to Galland, reached "80 per month." At that time, the *Staffeln* of JG 400 had around 140 aircraft on strength, although only some 40 pilots, while the specialist training *Gruppe* IV./EJG 2 was carrying out training to a sufficient standard up to the point of flight in an Me 163. The problem was that a shortage of the specialist fuel, particularly *C-Stoff* in the fall of 1944, precluded further training. Even if all available fuel had been diverted to the Me 163 training program, only ten pilots per month could have been trained, but that would have meant that there would have been insufficient fuel for JG 400 to fly missions.

America's industrial might – male and female employees on the assembly line at Boeing's Seattle plant work on the fuselages of B-17Fs in December 1942. (Library of Congress)

While under interrogation by Allied intelligence officers shortly after the war, Galland stated that he had, for a long time, "objected violently" to using rocket fuels for experimental development of new Flak weapons, high-speed submarines and other "exotica." He argued that the Me 163 had been what he described as "a reality," while the aforementioned weapon designs were pipe dreams. However, by the time the aircraft became available in numbers, even Späte questioned the rationale of full operational deployment of the Me 163, for as he wrote:

It was rather clear to me that the situation on all fronts had deteriorated to such an extent that employment of the few Me 163s we had would be rather meaningless.

AFTERMATH

By July 1944, the Allied bombing offensive had struck at every major synthetic plant in Germany. But Allied aircrews viewed a mission to the Leuna oil refining plant as the most dangerous and difficult they would undertake, for not only did it have the greatest concentration of Flak protection in Europe in the summer of 1944, by the fall, the threat of new Me 163 interceptors based close to the plant heightened the sense of danger. Despite several successful Allied attacks on the plant from July to September that caused either shut-down or significant damage and disruption to production, output was restored in mid-October, although it was at only nine percent of normal capacity. By December, according to Albert Speer, this shortfall in supply had reached 'catastrophic proportions' and meant that reserves for German operations in the Ardennes were woefully insufficient.

The problem was that the Luftwaffe simply did not have enough fighters to defend the plants.

Work had commenced back in 1941 on an "Me 163C" which was intended to solve the problem of the limited fuel load carried by the B-model by adding an auxiliary rocket motor which, although producing less thrust than the main engine, did not consume so much fuel. This would mean that the Me 163C could fly under power for 12 minutes – six minutes longer than the B-model. Furthermore, the cumbersome take-off dolly and landing skid design would be replaced by a retractable undercarriage. Both these enhancements required a lengthened fuselage. However, delays at Messerschmitt opened the door for Junkers at Dessau to become involved, and the project received the designation Ju 248. The Ju 248 V1 took to the air on February 8, 1945, but despite flight-testing, the design did not progress beyond initial development.

On April 10 orders were issued for I./JG 400 to commence conversion to the planned Horten H.VII (RLM designation 8-226) or the advanced Ho 229 flying wing

An RAF technical intelligence officer surveys the wreckage of an overturned Me 163B at Bad Zwischenahn in May 1945 – one of five such aircraft found destroyed in the eastern area of the airfield. The interceptor's undercarriage dolly and skid are still attached, but the cockpit and nose section have been smashed away and the tail assembly and Walter rocket motor are missing. (EN Archive)

jet fighter, but this came to nought. Meanwhile, the principle of rocket propulsion was adopted by Erich Bachem for his Ba 349 *Natter* VTO rocket point interceptor, which required launching from a purpose-built, 20m-tall tower or wooden pole. Built primarily of wood, like the Me 163, it was planned for the *Natter* to climb at high speed powered by a Walter HWK 109-509 A1 rocket motor. It would then be flown toward a bomber formation, at which the pilot would fire off a salvo of 30mm cannon shells or 55mm rockets. Weapons expended, he would eject and parachute back to the ground. The fundamental purpose of the *Natter* was to destroy at least one bomber during its mission, but work did not progress beyond the initial manned prototype in which the test pilot was killed.

FURTHER READING

BOOKS

Bowman, Martin, *Osprey Combat Aircraft 18 – B-17 Flying Fortress Units of the Eighth Air Force* (Part 1) (Osprey Publishing, 2000)

Caldwell, Donald, *Day Fighters in Defence of the Reich – A War Diary, 1942–45* (Frontline Books, 2011)

Clarke, R. M. (ed), *Boeing B-17 and B-29 Fortress and Superfortress Portfolio* (Brooklands Books, 1986)

Craven, W. F. and Cate, J. L., *The Army Air Forces in World War II, Volume I – Plans and Early Operations (January 1939 to August 1942)* (The University of Chicago Press, 1948)

Ebert, Hans J., Kaiser, Johann B. and Peters, Klaus, *Willy Messerschmitt – Pioneer of Aviation Design* (Schiffer Publishing, 1999)

Ethell, Jeffrey L., *Komet – The Messerschmitt 163* (Sky Books Press, 1978)

Freeman, Roger, *The US Strategic Bomber* (Macdonald and Jane's Publishing, 1975)

Freeman, Roger, *B-17 Flying Fortress* (Jane's Publishing, 1983)

Gooden, Brett, *Natter – Manned Missile of the Third Reich: Historic Step to Human Spaceflight* (self-published, 2019)

Holden, Nigel, *Gerhard Fieseler – The Man Behind the Storch* (Helion and Company, 2017)

Jablonski, Edward, *Flying Fortress – The Illustrated Biography of the B-17s and the Men Who Flew Them* (Echo Point Books and Media LLC, 2014)

Ransom, Stephen and Cammann, Hans-Hermann, *Me 163 – Rocket Interceptor* (Crécy Publishing, 2021)

Ransom, Stephen and Cammann, Hans-Hermann, *Osprey Aviation Elite Units 37 – Jagdgeschwader 400 – Germany's Elite Rocket Fighters* (Osprey Publishing, 2010)

Späte, Wolfgang, *Top Secret Bird – The Luftwaffe's Me 163 Comet* (Independent Books, 1995)

Stüwe, Botho, *Peenemünde West – Der Erprobungsstelle der Luftwaffe für geheime Fernlenkwaffen und deren Entwicklungsgeschichte* (Bechtermünz Verlag, 1998)

WEBSITES

Koos, Volker, *Heinkel He 176 – Dichtung und Wahrheit*, Arbeitsgemeinschaft Dt. Luftfahrthistorik, at https://adl-luftfahrthistorik.de/dok/heinkel-he-176-raketenflugzeug.pdf, published March 2019

Me 163B Komet at https://robdebie.home.xs4all.nl/me163.htm

The Hellmuth Walter Website at www.walterwerke.co.uk

457th Bomb Group – The Fireball Outfit at https://457thbombgroupassoc.org

INDEX

Page numbers in **bold** refer to illustrations. Some caption locators are in brackets.